The Catholic Biblical School Pro

M000104715

YEAR TWO

NEW TESTAMENT FOUNDATIONS: JESUS AND DISCIPLESHIP

TEACHER GUIDEBOOK

Prepared by
Angelo G. Giuliano, Judith A. Hubert, Dorothy Jonaitis, and Brian Schmisek

PAULIST PRESS
New York/Mahwah, NJ

Acknowledgments

Special thanks is given to Mary Ingenthron for the biblical drawings that are included throughout this book.

The scripture quotations contained herein are from the New Revised Standard Version: Catholic Edition Copyright © 1989 and 1993, by the Division of Christian Education of the National Council of the Churches of Christ in the United States of America. Used by permission. All rights reserved.

Cover design by Sharyn Banks

Book design by Celine Allen

Nihil Obstat: Rev. Msgr. Glenn D. Gardner
                        Censor Librorum

Imprimatur: + Most Reverend Kevin J. Farrell
                        Bishop of Dallas

April 2, 2008

The *Nihil Obstat* and *Imprimatur* are official declarations that the material reviewed is free of doctrinal or moral error. No implication is contained therein that those granting the *Nihil Obstat* and *Imprimatur* agree with the contents, opinions, or statements expressed.

Copyright © 2008 by Paulist Press, Inc.

All rights reserved. No part of this book may be reproduced or transmitted in any form or by any means, electronic or mechanical, including photocopying, recording or by any information storage and retrieval system without permission in writing from the publisher.

Permission is granted to teachers of these materials to reproduce for their students "Suggested Answers" and "Unit Exams."

ISBN: 978-0-8091-9587-9

Published by Paulist Press
997 Macarthur Boulevard
Mahwah, New Jersey 07430

www.paulistpress.com

Printed and bound in the
United States of America

Dedication

It is with respect and gratitude that this revision of *The Denver Catholic Biblical School Program* is dedicated to Sister Macrina Scott, OSF. It was her recognition of the need for a serious Bible study for the Catholic laity that led to the creation of the Catholic Biblical School in 1982. As the founder and for twenty years director of the school, Sister Macrina is a leader in the area of adult Catholic biblical literacy. We are grateful to her for the great gift that she has given to the church.

Because of her vision and determination, literally thousands of Catholics have had their eyes and hearts opened to the word and have grown in faith and knowledge, deepening their relationship with God through their study of scripture. With the publication of the Biblical School materials by Paulist Press beginning in 1994, Sister Macrina's dream bore fruit throughout the country. It is our hope that these revisions, renamed *The Catholic Biblical School Program*, will keep that dream alive well into the twenty-first century.

In addition, we would be remiss not to acknowledge the significant contributions of Steve Mueller, PhD, to the development of the original Biblical School program. We also remember Mary E. Ingenthron, now deceased, whose delightful illustrations grace this book.

Contents

Foreword

Welcome to the Catholic Biblical School Program. In the Catholic Church, sacred scripture is often called "the soul of theology." The study of sacred scripture on the part of Catholics reached new levels after Vatican II. Many programs have arisen since to meet the need. One was the Denver Catholic Biblical School more than twenty-five years ago. Since that time, the program has flourished in many places throughout the United States and beyond. One reason for the program's success is that it incorporates the fruit of the "indispensable method" of historical-criticism into the rich faith tradition of the church and the lives of the students.

As dean of the University of Dallas School of Ministry, I was elated when we were able to hire first Mr. Gene Giuliano, then Sr. Dorothy Jonaitis, and finally Ms. Angeline Hubert. Each of them is an acknowledged author of the "original" materials in the Denver Catholic Biblical School, and each of them taught there for a time. Now as faculty members at the Catholic Biblical School of the School of Ministry, they bring significant experience to their writing.

With this revision, we incorporated lessons learned from scholarship, from classroom teaching (our own and that of others), from updated materials, including the *Catechism of the Catholic Church* and statements from the Pontifical Biblical Commission, and from our own growth in spirituality and faith. We present the product of countless hours of discussion, prayer, and scholarly debate.

By using this workbook, you will become more familiar with the Bible. You will learn about its stories, its characters, its places, its themes, its promises, and its hopes. This sacred text will meet you in your own life, with your cares, concerns, worries, hopes, ambitions, and faith life. The sacred is something that exhausts us. We do not exhaust it. Time and again we approach it anew, whether we are seventeen or seventy-seven. We encourage you on your path to learning more about the sacred text, its inspired character, and its primary author. We hope you will find the workbook material nourishing both academically and spiritually.

Brian Schmisek, PhD
Dean, School of Ministry
University of Dallas

Introduction

Welcome back to your work as a guide on the journey of biblical discovery! As you know from working with the first year of this program, *Old Testament Foundations: Genesis through Kings*, this journey can be as exciting for you as it is for your students. You will continue to learn a great deal—much of it from your students.

Throughout the journey it is essential to keep in view the goal, which is to lead the participants into an experience of God's word as alive and able to change their lives. By returning regularly to this goal you will avoid wasting time on the many distracting and discouraging bypaths that offer themselves along the way.

As you know, the four-year plan for this program provides a map by which to guide your course (see page 97). Many years of experience have gone into this arrangement of the books of the Bible and general biblical topics. By following this plan you will ensure that the students' time is used to the best advantage with no essential items omitted and no time wasted on unnecessary repetition.

Overview of the Second Year

The second year of the program moves from the study of the Old Testament to a study of the New Testament. The year focuses on the questions, "Who is Jesus?" and "What does it mean to be his disciple?" Often students begin this year with a false sense of security. They are leaving the more unfamiliar material of the Old Testament for something that they think they understand. But they are surprised to discover new and more challenging dimensions in these books that they thought they knew.

Unit One

In the first unit of year two the students study the synoptic gospels of Mark and Luke. These familiar gospels are presented in the light of the teachings of Vatican II and of contemporary biblical scholarship. The students are introduced to the process of gospel formation as it is described in *Dei Verbum* §19. They discover that the gospels are not eye-witness presentations of Jesus' ministry. Rather, the gospels are proclamations of the good news of our salvation in Jesus as shaped by the creative work of each evangelist in response to the needs of his community.

The uniqueness of each gospel is stressed as the students explore the specific structure, themes, and theology of Mark and Luke. The use of the *Synopsis of the Four Gospels* is an indispensable tool for discovering the unique contributions of each evangelist and for approaching the synoptic question. Most students find the study of the gospels to be an exciting and eye-opening experience.

Unit Two

Unit two continues the study of Luke by exploring his second volume, the Acts of the Apostles. It then shifts to the letters of Paul. Students often find the study of Paul to be one of the most difficult parts of the Catholic Biblical School Program. With these letters, students for the first time encounter texts that are not narratives, which necessitates a shift in their approach to reading. Even though the letters are short, they are challenging because Paul's theology is difficult to grasp.

The students see Paul in his roles of pastor, theologian, and author. As a pastor, he wrote letters that were meant to solve real problems that confronted his communities in the 50s and 60s of the first century. As a theologian, he shaped a vision of what life in response to Christ's resurrection entailed. As an author, he used rhetorical skills common to ancient speakers and writers in order to persuade his readers.

Unit Three
The unit begins with the study of John's gospel and the Johannine letters. Having studied Mark and Luke-Acts, the students can appreciate the differences that John presents both in literary style and in theological content. They learn more about the historical situation of the early Christian communities in relation to the Jewish people. Stressing the unique structure, theology, and themes of John's gospel also serves to reinforce the uniqueness of the synoptics. The study of the three letters of John that follows the exploration of the gospel gives the students an insight into the problems faced by the next generation of the Johannine community.

Finally, the unit moves to the apocalyptic sections of the synoptic gospels and the Book of Revelation. If students cannot make the full four-year commitment to the program, a natural cut-off point is the end of the second year. That is why the Book of Revelation has been included here, to familiarize the students with it. By becoming familiar with the apocalyptic style of writing and with the historical situation of the Christian communities at the time of this book's writing, the students can discover the purpose and meaning that the author intended to communicate. The recognition that this is a literature of hope will help the students to confront its sometimes bizarre usage in our modern society.

The mix of materials covered in the second year provides a basic overview of the types of literature found in the New Testament: gospels (synoptics and John), letters, the more documentary or historical narration of Acts of the Apostles, and apocalyptic literature.

As you study the New Testament, look for opportunities to make connections between what the students are studying and what they have already studied in the Old Testament. This will enable them to see ways in which the New Testament fulfills the Old.

Use of These Materials

First of all, these materials were developed for groups of adults. One could use the questions for personal study, but the sharing of knowledge and faith by the students is important for their learning. The group process not only bonds the students into communities of learning, but also reinforces the idea that we all learn from one another, since each of us can be a source of insight and encouragement.

Second, while some programs can be led by just about anyone, this program is most effectively taught by a qualified teacher who has significant background in scripture. The role of the teacher as facilitator of the whole experience of scripture study cannot be underestimated. While studies show that adults thrive in self-directed study situations, the teacher is surely a helpful influence. The instructor not only models what it means to be a student of scripture, but he or she also acts as an on-the-spot resource person.

Third, the program includes that often neglected component of so much adult education, homework. So many programs rely solely on reading and discussion and do not assign any homework. When this program started, many people thought that adults would not put up with the demand of weekly homework. Well, they were wrong! Not only have students appreciated their assignments, but they have learned more effectively through their writing. Written homework makes the students more responsible in their reading and study of the material. But, more than anything else, the discipline of formulating a written answer compels the students to carefully think through their answers. Unlike some spoken discussions, a written answer cannot wander around interminably and is very helpful for the small group discussion. Written answers also encourage the introverts who are often likely to remain quiet in the midst of free-flowing group discussion.

Format for the Weekly Class

A weekly two-hour class is suggested, but the class format can be tailored to the needs of your community. For example, in some areas of the country, the class meets only once a month, with three lessons offered on a Saturday. The weekly class time involves an opening prayer, small group discussion of the homework assignments, a chance to address questions that have arisen, and a lecture by the teacher on the material to be studied for the coming week's lesson. This format provides a good balance between the students' discussion and their listening to the teacher's lecture.

The class time is divided up in this way:

5–10 minutes: Opening Prayer (prepared and led by students on a rotating basis)

5 minutes: Announcements

45–50 minutes: Small Group Discussion (students share written homework answers)

5–10 minutes: Student Questions and General Group Discussion

45–50 minutes: Teacher's Preview Lecture (on material to be studied for the coming week)

At the start of the year, students are assigned to a discussion group of six to eight students, and they generally stay in their assigned group for the entire year. Each week a different member of the group acts as the facilitator of the discussion. This experience gives the students a chance to develop some skill in leading a Bible discussion group.

Note that the teacher always lectures on the material that the students will be studying during the coming week. For example, the suggested lecture topics under Lesson II.3 should be given to prepare students for Assignment II.3. This preview gives the students an orientation and a context so that they are able to get the most out of their own reading and study. The teacher can supply much of the background material that the students need for their homework assignment.

At the end of class, teachers collect the weekly homework assignments and review them. Since the students have worked hard preparing their answers, the teacher ought to take time to carefully review and comment on their papers. The instructor needs to be on the lookout for students who are having problems interpreting the texts or making improper applications with regard to church doctrine. It is important to make encouraging comments on the students' papers, but error and inadequate interpretation cannot go unchallenged. Reading the papers each week takes time, but it enables you get to know each of the students through their weekly work.

Textbooks are used to supplement careful reading of the biblical texts. These are listed at the start of each unit in the student workbook. Although the textbooks are helpful, it is important to stress that the answers to the questions, unless a question specifically states otherwise, are to be found in the Bible and not in commentaries or textbooks.

Basic Principles

There are several underlying assumptions on which this program is based:

1. The entire Bible is inspired and normative for Christian faith. Individual parts must be understood in relation to the whole, not in isolation. As Vatican II's Dogmatic Constitution on Divine Revelation (*Dei Verbum*) reminds us: "God, the inspirer and author of both testaments, wisely arranged that the New Testament be hidden in

the Old and the Old be manifest in the New" (§16). The value of studying the entire Bible is that each of us is stretched in new ways by the parts we might not choose to study.

2. Adults need to be actively involved in their learning. The purpose of the lectures is to assist students in their own search for answers. Student opinions and experiences must be taken seriously as part of the educational process.

3. Scripture addresses the total human person. Therefore, the teaching of it should utilize right-brain and left-brain approaches in as great a variety as possible, using a range of formats, including:
- Personal study guided by questions
- Group discussion
- Lecture
- Tests
- Creative activities, including art, music, poetry, etc.
- Memorization of verses
- Audiovisual aids

4. Adults deserve the best that scholarship has to offer. Their time is too valuable to be spent reading or listening to outdated information.

Advice for the Teacher

Your most valuable asset in guiding the journey is your own prayerful reflection on scripture. If God's word is alive and active in you, you will be more likely to pass it on to your students as a living word.

A second asset is your knowledge of scripture and, to a lesser extent, of related areas such as church history and theology. The information that you communicate to your students is only a small portion of what you need to know in order to teach effectively. As long as you teach, you need to continue renewing and updating your biblical education. You cannot be content with the basic knowledge that you pass on to your students. You are fortunate if you work on a team or are in contact with peers who can share your study.

Honesty is another essential quality for you as teacher. Many students want simple, easy answers, but the Bible does not provide them. Instead, it serves as a challenge and guide. Its difficulty is such that on many points there is a wide variety of scholarly opinions. Recognize the difficulty and the diversity of the Bible honestly. Do not allow your students to read simply what they want into the text. In the same way, do not impose your own agenda on the biblical text. If you are not honest with the text, you cannot teach your students to be honest with the text.

You also need to understand your students. If you listen to them and read their papers carefully each week, you will come to know each of your students individually. You will find that many of them share these common characteristics of adult Catholic Bible students.

1. They are often unsure of themselves as students, and especially as students of the Bible. It is important that you read their homework papers each week and affirm the students for what they have done well, which is usually much more than they realize. If you correct them on matters that have nothing to do with the content of the program, such as grammar and spelling, you run the risk of turning them away from biblical study.

2. They sometimes find it difficult to remember the material taught. It is helpful if you return to major ideas frequently in your lecture, handouts, questions, and review sheets. At every opportunity, review previously studied material by connecting it with new material.

3. Their real interest is often the message of the scripture for their own lives. Help them see that

this includes not only their personal and family life, but also their parish community, their liturgical experience, and their lives as citizens. Avoid the types of scholarly debates that have little potential for application.

4. They are able to find the meaning of the text for their own lives, and may do so in ways that will surprise you. Many students have reported how powerful a lesson was in enabling them to deal with some personal crisis. Once the word of God is opened to them, they will find its application. Avoid imposing your interpretations in a way that might stifle their own encounter with the word.

5. They want to be challenged. When this program was planned, many professional educators said that it was much too demanding and that "Catholics aren't ready for anything like this." But, from the beginning, the response has been overwhelming. Individual students may try unsuccessfully to evade requirements and resist their firm application. But, in the end, they will be grateful for the requirements. They will know that they have learned more thoroughly than they could have without the strict requirements of the program.

6. They are able to learn from modern scholarship if it is presented to them carefully, avoiding jargon and controversies that do not really affect the core meaning of a text. It is the teacher's responsibility to assimilate the scholarly material and present the consensus as well as the church's teaching on scripture in language that makes it clear and applicable to real life.

Your preparation will enable you to enter into this adventure with enthusiasm. Those who have taught this program have found it among the most challenging and enriching experiences of their lives.

Student Workbook and Teacher Guidebook

This teacher guidebook is meant to be used in connection with the student workbook. It does not reproduce the materials in the student workbook that each student will purchase. You will need to have a copy of the student workbook to familiarize yourself with its format and contents.

For each lesson, the student workbook contains the study objectives, a reading assignment, a geography task, important terms, written work, optional challenge questions, a suggested memory verse, and suggestions for further reading. Supplementary Readings are provided at the end of the student workbook and are keyed to various lessons.

For each lesson, the teacher guidebook contains materials specifically for you as teacher. Besides a listing of the assigned readings from the Bible and the textbooks, these include:

Assignment Objectives that focus the material for your presentation.

Rationale for Student Questions that explains the purpose of each question that is asked of the students. The numbering of this section corresponds to the written work in the student workbook.

Suggested Lecture Topics that are meant to be suggestions, not an outline of what you will present. Every teacher will organize his or her lecture in a unique way. The suggested topics are especially related to the materials in the lesson.

Suggested Answers that are keyed to the student questions. You might wish to copy these answers for the students, or you could make one copy for each group to have during its discussion of the homework assignment. The suggested answers do not attempt to be exhaustive. *Note that no answers are provided for questions that ask for the students' opinions or for a creative response.* The suggested answers focus the students' attention on the basic information that they can discover in their reading and study, but they often find different answers for the questions.

Unit Tests that can be duplicated and used to evaluate the students' progress. The unit test provides an opportunity for integration of the assigned materials, assimilation of the basic information that every student of the Bible should know, and accountability for the content of what has been taught in the unit. The main work of the unit has already been completed when the students turn in their weekly written assignments. The test is not comprehensive, but rather a way to solidify the basic information that the students need to know.

It is hoped that these materials will help you as you lead others to the mystery of The One who is revealed to us through reading and studying the sacred texts. As you lead others on the journey, remember the question posed by the deacon Philip and the wonderful answer of the Ethiopian eunuch (Acts 8:30–31):

> Do you understand what you are reading?
> How can I, unless someone guides me?

UNIT I
Jesus: Two Synoptic Views

Objectives

To enable students:

1. To recall the chronology, geography, and historical-social environment of New Testament Christianity.

2. To recognize the Christian message in its narrative presentation (gospel) through an investigation of the structure, sources, themes, and theologies of Mark and Luke.

3. To analyze the gospels of Mark and Luke using the historical-critical method, including literary criticism, form criticism, and redaction criticism.

4. To use the gospels of Mark and Luke for personal and communal prayer.

Textbooks

Primary Text: The Bible. Use a good translation with scholarly notes.

Other Texts: For helpful background and handy reference we recommend:
  Eerdmans *Dictionary of the Bible* (cited as EDB)
  Hammond's *Atlas of the Bible Lands* (cited as Hammond Atlas)
  Kurt Aland, ed., *Synopsis of the Four Gospels*
  Joseph F. Kelly, *An Introduction to the New Testament for Catholics* (cited as Kelly)

Assignments

Each lesson is to be studied by the students in preparation for their group discussion. For each biblical passage, students study the biblical text and footnotes for that particular passage, do other assigned readings, and answer the written work *on a separate page.*

      I.1   APPROACHING THE GOSPELS

      I.2   MARK 1–3

      I.3   MARK 4:1—8:21

      I.4   MARK 8:22—13:37

      I.5   MARK 14–16

      I.6   INFANCY NARRATIVES: LUKE 1–2; MATTHEW 1–2

      I.7   LUKE 3:1—9:50

      I.8   LUKE 9:51—19:27

      I.9   LUKE 19:28—24:53

      I.10 UNIT ONE REVIEW

      UNIT ONE TEST

- mail Craig
- get new checks
- Set up box for B. Stday.
- plact fr. fr. invoice
- e-mail N. Dawson

nldawsonphd@

I.1
Approaching the Gospels

Assignment Objectives

To enable students:

1. To describe the three stages of gospel formation.

2. To explain the key role of human authors and their contribution to the process of gospel formation.

3. To recognize that the same gospel content can be presented in many forms.

4. To recall that the literary form of the gospels is the narrative proclamation of the good news of our Christian salvation.

5. To recognize that the gospels reflect the Christian community's faith interpretation and application of the events concerning Jesus Christ.

6. To locate the kingdom of Herod, the Sea of Galilee, the Jordan River, the Dead Sea, Judea, Samaria, and the Roman provinces of Syria, Galatia, Asia, and Macedonia on a map.

Read

Kelly, pages 18–30 and 80–88; EDB article: "Jesus Christ: Sources"; "Truth and Its Many Expressions," #1, and "The Three Stages of the Composition of the Gospels (Vatican II)," #2, in the SUPPLEMENTARY READINGS at the back of the student workbook

Rationale for Student Questions

1. To become acquainted with the Catholic approach to biblical interpretation as found in Vatican II's Dogmatic Constitution on Divine Revelation (*Dei Verbum*).

2. To understand the process of gospel formation.

3. To recognize the importance of looking for the meaning of the events in scripture by exploring the importance of the meaning of events in their own lives.

4. To reflect more deeply on the church's teachings about biblical interpretation.

5. To recognize the importance of the historical context of the gospels.

Suggested Lecture Topics

– Development of the New Testament canon.

– Introduction to the literary form of gospel.

– Three stages of gospel formation as described in *Dei Verbum*, §19.

– Gospel as a faith account of the Christian community's interpretation of the meaning of Jesus' life.

– The different portrayals of Jesus and discipleship in the gospels due to different ways of presenting the Christian message to church communities in different cultures and different situations.

– Koine Greek—the written language of the New Testament.

SUGGESTED ANSWERS FOR UNIT I.1

1. According to Vatican II's Dogmatic Constitution on Divine Revelation (*Dei Verbum*), authentic biblical interpretation takes place in the context of the teaching authority of the church under the guidance of the Holy Spirit. Catholics believe that the biblical texts were written under the inspiration of that same Spirit for the sake of salvation. The church also affirms that God spoke through human authors and that, in order to properly interpret scripture, we must "investigate what meaning the sacred authors really intended, and what God wanted to manifest by their words" (*Dei Verbum*, §19). It is essential that the interpreter recognize and respect the literary form in which the scripture text is written as well as its historical and cultural context. The whole Bible and the living tradition of the church must be considered when interpreting the sacred texts.

2. The three stages of gospel formation:

   a. The lived stage: The actual events of Jesus' life and the actual words he preached.

   b. The oral stage: The preaching and teaching of the apostles after the ascension of Jesus.

   c. The written stage: The gospel material as it exists in the four gospels. The words of Jesus and accounts of his deeds were synthesized and organized into written documents by the evangelists in order to address the situations of their own communities at the time of the writing of the gospel texts.

Christians confessed that "on a set day they used to meet before dawn and sing a hymn among themselves to Christ, as though he were a god."

—Letter (X.25 ff) from Pliny to the Emperor Trajan (about AD 112)

Assignment Objectives

To enable students:

1. To note that the gospels revolve around two major questions:

   a. Who is Jesus?

   b. What does it mean to be Jesus' disciple?

2. To identify understanding/misunderstanding as a key Markan theme.

3. To recognize the two-part structure of Mark's gospel.

4. To explain Markan priority and the two-source hypothesis regarding the synoptic problem.

5. To use the *Synopsis of the Four Gospels* to compare and contrast parallel gospel texts.

Read

Mark 1–3; Kelly, pages 89–96; EDB articles: "Messiah," "Q," and "Son of God"; "The Synoptic Gospels and Their Sources," #3, "Exploring the Synoptic Gospels: Mark and His Careful Readers," #4, and "The Gospel According to Mark: Overview," #5, in the SUPPLEMENTARY READINGS at the back of the student workbook

Rationale for Student Questions

To enable students:

1. To see and become familiar with Mark's portrait of Jesus.
2. To recognize the role of call in Christian discipleship and to reflect upon its meaning in their lives.
3. To discover the uniqueness of each of the synoptic gospels.
4. To consider Mark's portrayal of the family of Jesus.
5. To trace the Markan theme of understanding/misunderstanding.

Suggested Lecture Topics

- Introduction to the synoptic question and the two-source hypothesis, i.e., Mark as the first written gospel, used along with the Q source by Matthew and Luke.
- Reinforcement of the importance of the three stages of gospel formation.
- Use of the *Synopsis of the Four Gospels.*
- Brief comparison of Mark with other synoptics to demonstrate that each gospel is a unique work.
- Introduction to Mark's gospel, its characteristics, structure, and setting.
- Mark's portrait of Jesus and understanding of discipleship.
- Introduction of Markan themes, especially understanding/misunderstanding.
- Similarities between Old Testament characters (e.g., Ahab/Jezebel/Elijah) and ones who appear in Mark (e.g., Herod/Herodias/John the Baptist).
- Meaning of the desert and temptation in the Old Testament as related to the temptations of Jesus.

SUGGESTED ANSWERS FOR UNIT I.2

1. a. Jesus is the Christ/Messiah and the Son of God.

   b. Jesus is:

      • Mightier than John the Baptist and will baptize with the Holy Spirit (Mark 1:7–8)

      • From Nazareth (Mark 1:9)

      • Baptized by John (Mark 1:9)

      • The Beloved Son (Mark 1:11)

      • One who must do battle with Satan (Mark 1:12–13)

      • Important enough to be ministered to by angels (Mark 1:13)

      • A preacher and proclaimer of the good news of God (Mark 1:14–15, 38–39)

      • Involved in the time of fulfillment/messianic time (Mark 1:15)

      • One who calls others to share in his ministry (Mark 1:16–20)

      • A teacher with authority (Mark 1:22, 27)

      • One who has power over unclean spirits and is the Holy One of God (Mark 1:24–27)

      • One who has power over illness (Mark 1:31–34, 40–42)

      • One who prays (Mark 1:35)

   c. Jesus:

      • Has authority to forgive sins and to heal (Mark 2:5–12)

      • Calls sinners and socializes with them (Mark 2:14–17)

      • Has authority to rescind the Jewish fasting law (Mark 2:18–20)

      • Has power/authority over the law of Sabbath observance (Mark 2:27–28 and 3:1–5)

2. a. A disciple:

      • Repents and believes the good news of God (Mark 1:15)

      • Immediately responds to the call of Jesus and leaves all behind to follow him (Mark 1:16–20; 2:14)

      • Shares an intimacy with Jesus (Mark 2:15–17)

      • Needs Jesus (Mark 2:17)

3. a. Significant ways in which Matthew and Luke differ from Mark:

      • Matthew and Luke omit Mark's comment "those whom he desired; and they came to him" (Mark 3:13b) and his comment that he called them "to be with him" (Mark 3:14b).

      • In Luke Jesus prays all night before he calls the twelve (Luke 6:12).

      • Luke and Matthew both refer to the twelve as apostles (Luke 6:13b and 10:2a). Some ancient authorities add "whom also he named apostles" to the Markan text.

- Matthew includes authority to heal (Matt 10:1c) and skips Mark's reference to "be sent out to preach" (Mark 3:14b).

- Luke omits Mark 3:14b–15.

- Matthew and Luke have several differences in the listing and description of the twelve. Among these differences, only Matthew's gospel refers to Matthew as a tax collector (Matt 10:3b) and Luke's gospel omits Thaddaeus and instead lists Judas the son of James (Luke 6:16a).

4. a. The family of Jesus is concerned that he has lost his mind, and they have come to restrain him (Mark 3:21). They are "standing outside" and not with those who are "sitting around him" (Mark 3:32). Jesus broadens the understanding of his family beyond the biological to include all who do "the will of God" (Mark 3:33–35).

5. Understanding/Misunderstanding

Reference in Mark	Who	U/M	Why Included
1:1	Author	U	He properly identifies Jesus as the Christ and Son of God.
1:7–8	John the Baptist	U	He calls Jesus "one who is more powerful…"
1:11	Voice from heaven	U	"You are my Son, the beloved; with you I am well pleased."
1:34	Demons	U	They knew him.
1:24	Unclean spirit	U	He calls Jesus the Holy One of God.
2:5	Friends of the paralytic	U	Jesus saw their faith.
2:6–7	Scribes	M	They think that Jesus is blaspheming.
3:6	Pharisees	M	They want to destroy him.
3:11	Unclean spirits	U	They say that he is the Son of God.
3:21	Relatives	M	They think that he has lost his mind.
3:22	Scribes	M	They say, "He has Beelzebul."
3:30	Scribes	M	They said, "He has an unclean spirit."

1.3
Mark 4:1—8:21

Assignment Objectives

To enable students:

1. To recognize the nature and purpose of parables in Mark's gospel.

2. To grasp Jesus' message concerning the kingdom of God and to note his challenges to the conventional morality of his time and culture.

3. To explain Mark's idea of the purpose and meaning of Jesus' miracles and the role they play in relation to the kingdom of God.

4. To recognize the universality of the kingdom of God as a Markan theme.

Read   Mark 4:1—8:21; Kelly, pages 96-98; EDB articles: "Kingdom of God," "Miracle," "Parable," and "Syrophoenician"

Rationale for Student Questions

To enable students:
1. To analyze the setting and content of the parable of the sower.
2. To note that the portrayal of Jesus and of his disciples is not the same in each gospel.
3. To apply the biblical text to their personal experience.
4. To examine a key Markan theme and to see how Mark develops this theme in his gospel.
5. To continue to trace the theme of understanding/misunderstanding.
6. To deepen their understanding of parables through a creative experience.

Suggested Lecture Topics

– Parables, their structure, purpose, challenge, and connection to the kingdom of God.

– Miracles in Jesus' ministry as signs of the coming of the kingdom of God.

– Role of faith as it is presented in the description of Jesus' miracles.

– Themes presented in the bread section (e.g., universality—the Christian community includes both Gentiles and Jews—and unity in community through the Eucharist [Mark 6:31—8:21]).

– Synoptic contrast between faith (as basic trust, not assent to doctrine) and fear.

SUGGESTED ANSWERS FOR UNIT I.3

1. a. Jesus addresses the parable to the crowd.

   b. Jesus explains the parable to "those who were around him along with the twelve" (Mark 4:10).

2. a. Significant ways in which Matthew and Luke differ from Mark:

   • Matthew says that the disciples followed Jesus onto the boat (Matt 8:23), while Mark says, "they took him with them" (Mark 4:36).

   • In Mark the disciples call Jesus "teacher" (Mark 4:38b). In Matthew they call him "Lord" (Matt 8:25a), and in Luke they call him "Master" (Luke 8:24).

   • In Mark the disciples ask Jesus, "Do you not care if we perish?" (Mark 4:38b), while in Matthew and Luke they simply say, "We are perishing" (Matt 8:25; Luke 8:24b).

   • In Mark Jesus asks the disciples "Have you no faith?" (Mark 4:40b). In Matthew he calls them "men of little faith" (Matt 8:26b), and in Luke he asks, "Where is your faith?" (Luke 8:25a).

   b. Matthew and Luke seem to soften Mark's portrayal of the disciples. The disciples follow Jesus, and they have a little or some faith rather than no faith. In Mark the disciples question whether Jesus cares about them, while in Matthew and Luke they simply describe their situation. Matthew's and Luke's references to Jesus as "Lord" or "Master" represent a heightened view of Jesus' identity.

4. Some examples of the theme of universality are:

   • Jesus and the disciples travel across the sea to the Gentile side, and Jesus exorcises the Gerasene demoniac (Mark 5:1–20).

   • Jesus goes back to the Jewish side of the sea and cures a woman with a hemorrhage (Mark 5:25–34).

   • Jesus raises the daughter of a Jewish synagogue ruler (Jairus) from the dead (Mark 5:21–24, 35–43) and also cures the daughter of the Syro-Phoenician woman (Mark 7:24–30).

   • Jesus multiplies loaves and fishes on both the Jewish side (Mark 6:35–44) and the Gentile side of the Sea of Galilee (Mark 8:1–10).

   • Jesus cures a deaf mute in the Decapolis (Gentile) region (Mark 7:31–37).

   • The building of the kingdom of God affects Gentiles as well as Jews (notice the tying-together effect of traveling from one side of the sea to the other), women as well as men, and the lowly (children) as well as the important (synagogue ruler).

5. Understanding/Misunderstanding
   See chart on next page

Reference in Mark	Who	U/M	Why Included
4:13	Disciples	M	They don't understand the parable.
4:38	Disciples	M	They think Jesus doesn't care.
5:7	Man with an unclean spirit	U	He calls Jesus "Son of the Most High God."
5:34	Woman with the hemorrhage	U	Jesus commends her faith.
6:2–3, 6	People of Nazareth	M	They lack faith in Jesus.
6:14–16	Herod and the people	M	They think that Jesus is John the Baptist.
6:49–52	Disciples	M	Their hearts were hardened.
7:18	Disciples	M	They failed to understand.
7:24–30	Syro-Phoenician woman	U	She persisted, knowing that Jesus could heal her daughter.
8:11	Pharisees	M	They were looking for a sign.
8:14–21	Disciples	M	They misunderstand what Jesus is saying.

I.4
Mark 8:22—13:37

Assignment Objectives

To enable students:

1. To recognize the general form of a miracle story and its function in Mark's gospel.

2. To detect the often used Markan technique of intercalation (framing).

3. To recognize the importance of Peter's profession as the climax of the first part of Mark's gospel and to see how it ushers in the second part of the gospel.

4. To understand Jesus' teachings on discipleship in Mark 8:27–13:37.

5. To specify the role of suffering in Jesus' ministry, particularly in Mark 8:27–13:37.

6. To see how Jesus' words and deeds in Jerusalem are a judgment on the Judaism of his time.

Read

Mark 8:22–13:37; Kelly, pages 99–103; EDB articles: "Eschatology: Jesus and the Gospels," "Son of Man," "Temple: Jerusalem Temple," and "Transfiguration"

Rationale for Student Questions

To enable the students:

1. To recognize the significance of miracles in relation to their location in the text.

2. To note the distinctions between the synoptic gospels.

3. To continue to explore Mark's portrayal of Jesus and of discipleship and to apply it to their experience of discipleship.

4. To discover Mark's intercalation technique.

5. To recognize an important title of Jesus and to reflect on its meaning.

6. To continue to trace the theme of understanding/misunderstanding.

Suggested Lecture Topics

- Significance of Peter's profession in Mark 8:27–33.

- Significance of the journey to Jerusalem in Mark's gospel.

- What Jesus' passion predictions and the teachings that follow them reveal about the identity of Jesus and the meaning of discipleship.

- Significance of the transfiguration.

- Mark's use of intercalation (framing).

- Jesus' judgment on Jerusalem in his actions and in his words.

- Background of Passover and the layers of meaning connected to this feast:
  • Shepherd's spring feast—lamb, blood on lintel
  • Farmer's spring feast—unleavened bread
  • Historical memories—the exodus from Egypt

- Christian Eucharist—blood of covenant, bread, exodus memory, and memory of Jesus.

SUGGESTED ANSWERS FOR UNIT I.4

1. Both are healing miracles curing blindness. Sight is often used as a symbol of faith or understanding and blindness often refers to a lack of faith or understanding. These two miracles illustrate Jesus' attempt to have his followers see, that is, understand who he is and also to understand what it means to be his follower. Note that Bartimaeus, who now sees, follows Jesus on the way (Mark 10:52).

2. a. Significant ways in which Matthew and Luke differ from Mark:

    • Luke prefaces this story with Jesus at prayer (Luke 9:18a).

    • In Matthew Jesus refers to himself as the "Son of Man" (Matt 16:13b), and Matthew includes Jeremiah among those who people say Jesus is (Matt 16:14b).

    • Matthew also adds the story of Peter becoming the rock on which the church is built. Only in Matthew is Peter given the keys to the kingdom of heaven and the authority to bind and loose (Matt 16:16–19).

    • While Luke omits the story about Peter rebuking Jesus, Matthew adds Peter's words of rebuke (Matt 16:22b) and has Jesus call him a hindrance or stumbling block (Matt 16:23b).

3. a. Mark sees Jesus as one who will suffer greatly through rejection, betrayal, and death and then ultimately rise (Mark 8:31; 9:31; 10:33–34). Jesus' life is one of service and his death a ransom for many (Mark 10:45).

    b. The disciple's life is also marked by suffering and self-denial. Disciples are to share in the fate of Jesus, taking up their cross (Mark 8:34). They are to be willing to give their lives for Jesus and for the sake of the gospel (Mark 8:35). Discipleship is not about status or greatness, but rather about service (Mark 9:35–36; 10:42–43).

5. According to Donald Senior in his EDB article "Son of Man," the term is used as a self-designation for Jesus. He points out that interpreters have divided the uses of the title into three categories:

    – Jesus within the context of his earthly ministry has the authority to forgive sins (Mark 2:10) and is lord of the Sabbath (Mark 2:28).

    – Humiliation and suffering of the Son of Man (the passion predictions [Mark 8:31; 9:31; 10:33]) and giving his life as a ransom for the many (Mark 9:12; 10:45).

    – Future coming in judgment (Mark 8:38).

6. Understanding/Misunderstanding
    See chart on next page

Reference in Mark	Who	U/M	Why Included
8:28	People	M	They don't know who Jesus is.
8:29	Peter	U	He recognizes that Jesus is the Messiah.
8:32–33	Peter	M	He rebukes Jesus.
9:20	Unclean spirit	U	He recognizes Jesus.
9:24	Boy's father	U	He proclaims his belief.
9:32	Disciples	M	They didn't understand and were afraid to ask.
10:37–39	James and John	M	They don't understand what they are asking.
10:47–52	Bartimaeus	U	His faith made him well.
11:18	Chief priests and scribes	M	They want to kill Jesus.
11:27–33	Chief priests, scribes, and elders	M	They question Jesus' authority.
12:13–17	Pharisees and Herodians	M	They try to trap Jesus.
12:32–34	Scribe	U	He answers wisely.

Most exegetes, if we may judge from the commentaries on Scripture, would be working with a definition of the literal sense closely resembling the following: The sense which the human author directly intended and which the written words conveyed.

—Raymond E. Brown, SS "Hermeneutics," *in* The New Jerome Biblical Commentary, 71:9

I.5
Mark 14–16

Assignment Objectives

To enable students:

1. To recognize that each passion narrative fits with the gospel in which it occurs.

2. To explain Mark's passion framework, distinctive themes, and theology.

3. To identify Mark's presentation of Jesus as the Suffering Son of Man.

4. To describe the Messiah from Mark's point of view and explain why Mark's portrait of Jesus was relevant to the needs of his community.

5. To recognize how Mark uses the Old Testament as a source for interpreting the meaning of the passion event (in particular, Psalm 22 and the Suffering Servant in Isaiah 50:4–9; 52:13—53:12).

6. To identify important sites in Jerusalem that existed during the time of Jesus.

Read   Mark 14–16; Kelly, pages 103–9; EDB articles: "Abba," "Lord's Supper: Matthew and Mark," "Passion Narratives," and "Pilate, Pontius"

Rationale for Student Questions

To enable students:
1. To identify one of the reversals found in Mark's passion narrative.
2. To make connections with the Old Testament and with their personal experience.
3. To observe the evangelist's use of the Old Testament as a way of clarifying and bringing meaning to the death of Jesus.
4. To continue to develop skill in using the *Synopsis of the Four Gospels*.
5. To see that the understanding/misunderstanding theme runs through the entire gospel.
6. To appreciate the need for all of the gospel versions and to feel the impact of Mark's version on their spiritual lives.

Suggested Lecture Topics

– Form, structure, and purpose of the passion narrative.

– Institution narrative/Eucharist.

– Unique elements of Mark's passion and resurrection narratives, illustrating his view of Jesus' identity and the meaning of Jesus' death and resurrection.

– Misunderstanding of Jesus magnified in Mark's passion narrative.

– Mark's use of Old Testament connections, particularly Psalm 22 and Isaiah's Suffering Servant, to interpret the meaning of the passion.

– Christian meaning of Jesus' death as a reversal of the conventional expectations of Judaism.

– Different endings to Mark's gospel.

SUGGESTED ANSWERS FOR UNIT I.5

1. Contrary to the expectations of a Messiah who would live and rule and restore Israel to its former glory, Jesus is anointed for suffering and death. He says of the woman, "She has anointed my body beforehand for its burial" (Mark 14:8). Jesus' passion, death, and ultimately his resurrection define his Messiahship.

2. a. Just as in Exodus 24 the blood of the sacrifice served as a ratification of God's covenant with the Israelites, so will the new covenant be ratified by the blood of Jesus. Earlier in the gospel Jesus spoke of giving his life as a "ransom for many" (Mark 10:45). Now, in Mark 14:24, he speaks of his blood "which is poured out for many."

3. Some parallels are:

   - Jesus cries out "My God, my God, why have you forsaken me?" (Mark 15:34 and Psalm 22:1[22:2 in NAB]).

   - Jesus is mocked and derided (Mark 15:16–20, 29–32 and Psalm 22:6–7 [22:7–8 in NAB]).

   - Jesus' clothing is divided through the casting of lots (Mark 15:24 and Psalm 22:18 [22:19 in NAB]).

   - Note also that while there might not be other exact references, some of the atmosphere and feeling brought out by Psalm 22 can be seen in Mark's passion narrative.

4. a. In Mark many false witnesses come forward and they don't agree. The charge by the false witnesses is "We heard him say, 'I will destroy this temple that is made with hands, and in three days I will build another, not made with hands'" (Mark 14:58). In Matthew the charge by the false witnesses is "This fellow said, 'I am able to destroy the temple of God, and to build it in three days'" (Matt 26:61). Luke does not mention the charges.

   b. In all three of the synoptic gospels, Jesus is asked if he is the Christ. His answer in Mark is the most direct: "I am" (Mark 14:62a). In both Matthew and Luke, his response is less direct. Jesus implies that the questioners have already made up their minds: "You have said so" (Matt 26:64a) and "You say that I am" (Luke 22:70). Jesus' response in Luke also shows the questioners' insincerity and lack of faith: "If I tell you, you will not believe; and if I ask you, you will not answer" (Luke 22:67b–68).

   In all three synoptic gospels, Jesus speaks of the Son of Man seated at the right hand of power (Mark 14:62b; Matt 26:64b; Luke 22:69). Mark and Matthew carry this possible allusion to Daniel 7:13 further with Jesus' reference to the Son of Man "coming on/with the clouds of heaven" (Mark 14:62c; Matt 26:64c).

5. Understanding/Misunderstanding
   See chart on next page

Reference in Mark	Who	U/M	Why Included
14:1	Chief priests and scribes	M	They want to kill Jesus.
14:3	Woman who anoints Jesus	U	She anoints his head.
14:4–5	People present	M	They think that the oil is wasted.
14:10–11	Judas Iscariot	M	He wants to betray Jesus.
14:37–41	Peter/James/John	M	They fall asleep and don't know what to say to Jesus.
14:44–45	Judas	M	He betrays Jesus.
14:50	Disciples	M	They desert Jesus and flee.
14:56–59	False witnesses	M	They falsely accuse Jesus.
14:64	High priest	M	He accuses Jesus of blasphemy.
14:65	Guards	M	They mock and beat Jesus.
14:68–71	Peter	M	He denies Jesus.
15:10–14	Chief priests and crowd	M	They want Barabbas released and Jesus crucified.
15:16–20	Soldiers	M	They mock Jesus.
15:29–30	Passers-by	M	They mock Jesus.
15:31–32	Chief priests and scribes	M	They mock Jesus.
15:32b	Two crucified with Jesus	M	They abuse Jesus.
15:39	Centurion	U	He recognizes that Jesus is the Son of God.
15:43	Joseph of Arimathea	U	He was waiting for the kingdom of God.
16:8	Women at the tomb	M	They are afraid and tell no one.

I.6
Infancy Narratives: Luke 1–2; Matthew 1–2

Assignment Objectives

To enable students:

1. To recognize that the infancy narratives serve as overtures to the gospels.

2. To articulate the distinctiveness and theological significance of the infancy narratives of Matthew and Luke.

3. To indicate how each narrative uses the Old Testament in the development of the story.

4. To recognize that the infancy narratives, like the gospels themselves, are not first historical but rather theological in their purpose.

Read

Matthew 1–2; Luke 1–2; Kelly, pages 114–17 and 136–41; EDB articles: "Dreams," "Gabriel," "Joseph #9," and "Mary #1"; "Luke-Acts: Overview," #8, and "How to Read the Nativity Stories of Jesus," #9, in the SUPPLEMENTARY READINGS at the back of the student workbook

Rationale for Student Questions

To enable students:

1. To analyze the infancy narratives of Luke and Matthew and to recognize the distinctiveness of each narrative.

2. To read the infancy narratives critically and to relate them to popular depictions of the Christmas story.

3. To become acquainted with the different themes of each infancy narrative and to see how these themes are reflected in each gospel.

4. To note the common elements of the two annunciation stories.

5. To recognize and trace the important Lukan theme of prayer through the narrative.

6. To make a personal connection with the infancy stories.

Suggested Lecture Topics

– Content, purpose, structure, and nature of the infancy narratives of Matthew and Luke.

– Basic similarities and differences between the infancy narratives of Matthew and Luke.

– Uniqueness of each version and its expression of the evangelist's theological purpose.

– Examples of other infancy narratives that were not accepted into the canon of the New Testament (e.g., "The Infancy Gospel of Thomas," in *Lost Scriptures*, by Bart D. Ehrman [Oxford University Press, 2003], 57–62).

– Importance of Jerusalem and the Jerusalem temple in the Old Testament.

SUGGESTED ANSWERS FOR UNIT I.6

1. Similarities and differences between the infancy narratives:

Luke	Matthew
a. i. Zechariah (1:11), Mary (1:27), shepherds (2:8) ii. The angel Gabriel (1:19), the angel Gabriel (1:26), an angel of the Lord (2:9) iii. John (1:13), Jesus (1:31), other titles are also added; no name is given, but the child is called a Savior, who is the Messiah, the Lord (2:11)	a. i. Joseph (1:20) ii. An angel of the Lord in a dream (1:20) iii. Jesus (1:21)
b. i. Neighbors and relatives of Elizabeth (1:58) ii. Jews, unclear if they were rich or poor i. Shepherds (2:16) ii. Unclear if they were Jews or Gentiles, rich or poor, but probably Jews from the local area and poor	b. i. Wise men from the East (2:1) ii. Gentiles, probably rich
c. Annunciation to Zechariah (1:8–23) The presentation (2:22–24) Simeon's proclamation concerning Jesus (2:25–35) Anna's speaking about Jesus (2:36–38) Finding of Jesus after three days (2:41–50)	c. None
d. While Luke has many Old Testament allusions, not once does he say an Old Testament prophecy is fulfilled.	d. Isaiah 7:14 in Matthew 1:22–23 Micah 5:2 (5:1 in NAB and NJB) in Matthew 2:5–6 Hosea 11:1 in Matthew 2:15 Jeremiah 31:15 in Matthew 2:17–18 He shall be called a Nazorean in Matthew 2:23 (not found in the Old Testament)
e. Elizabeth, Mary, and Anna	e. Mary is the only one who plays an active part. However, women are mentioned in the genealogy: Tamar, Rahab, Ruth, Uriah's wife (Bathsheba).

2. Familiar Christmas images found in the gospels:

Luke		Matthew	
a.	1:27, 34	a.	1:18–25
b.	2:13–14	b.	Not mentioned
c.	1:31	c.	1:21
d.	2:39–40	d.	2:23
e.	Not mentioned	e.	Not mentioned
f.	1:30–35	f.	1:20–23
g.	Not mentioned	g.	2:16–18
h.	1:27, 34	h.	1:23
i.	Not mentioned	i.	2:2
j.	1:27, 32	j.	1:16, 20
k.	Not mentioned	k.	Not mentioned
l.	2:5–6	l.	1:24–25
m.	1:35	m.	1:18, 20
n.	2:7, 12, 16	n.	Not mentioned
o.	2:11	o.	1:21
p.	Not mentioned	p.	2:13–15
q.	1:5	q.	2:1
r.	Not mentioned	r.	Not mentioned
s.	2:4–6	s.	2:1

3. Many members of Matthew's community were Jewish converts, so he stressed that Jesus was the fulfillment of Old Testament prophecies. He also paralleled Jesus' life with that of Moses. Jesus, like Moses, escaped the slaughter of baby boys and came out of Egypt. Like the Jewish members of Matthew's community who had been rejected by the Jewish authorities, so too Jesus was rejected and threatened by Herod. Matthew's community also had Gentile members and his infancy narrative shows openness to Gentiles. The Gentile magi believed in Jesus and came to worship him (prefiguring the mission to the Gentiles [Matt 28:19–20]), while Matthew tells us that "all Jerusalem" feared Jesus. Joseph took Jesus to Egypt, a Gentile land, for safety.

Prayer is a major theme in Luke's gospel. This theme is reflected in the beautiful canticles of Zechariah, Mary, and Simeon and in the proclamation of the angels to the shepherds. Luke emphasizes the proper use of wealth and responsibility to the poor. In his gospel, Jesus was born not in a house but in a manger; his first visitors were poor shepherds, not wealthy magi with expensive gifts, and his parents presented the offering of the poor in the temple. Luke also focuses on the temple. The narrative begins with Zechariah offering sacrifice in the temple. Mary and Joseph took Jesus there as an infant and again when he was twelve.

4. Annunciation stories:

Common Elements	Luke 1:5–23	Luke 1:26–38
Angel Gabriel appears	1:11, 19	1:26–27
Startled reaction	1:12	1:29
Told not to fear	1:13	1:30
Addressed by name	1:13	1:30
Birth of a son is foretold and the son is named	1:13	1:31
Objection is raised	1:18	1:34
Child will be great	1:15–17	1:32–33, 35
Sign is given	1: 20	1:36–37

5. Prayer

Reference in Luke	Who Prays	Content
1:10	The full assembly	Not given
1:13	Zechariah	For a son
1:46–55	Mary	Praised God in joy, humility, and faith for what he does for the lowly
1:68–79	Zechariah	Praised and thanked God for his son
2:13–14	Angels	Glorified God in joy for the birth of Jesus
2:20	Shepherds	Praised and glorified God for what they had heard and seen
2:28–32	Simeon	Praised and thanked God for fulfilling his promise
2:37	Anna	Worshiped God
2:38	Anna	Praised God for Jesus

Luke's account of the conception, birth, and infancy of Jesus is one of his finest creations. There was nothing in Mark's Gospel to guide him. Matthew has an infancy narrative, but there is every indication that Luke and Matthew had no knowledge of each other's work. Rather, they composed their account separately at a time when the church was reflecting back beyond Jesus' public ministry to his earthly beginnings.

—Jerome Kodell, OSB, "Luke," in The Collegeville Bible Commentary

I.7
Luke 3:1—9:50

Assignment Objectives

To enable students:

1. To recall §19 of Vatican II's Dogmatic Constitution on Divine Revelation (*Dei Verbum*) on the three stages of gospel formation.

2. To note how Luke adapted Mark's gospel for his own purposes.

3. To apply the methods of redaction criticism to discover the evangelist's work as an editor.

4. To recognize the uniqueness of Luke's gospel, its structure, themes, and emphases concerning Jesus and discipleship.

5. To identify Lukan themes: fulfillment, salvation history, discipleship, prayer, Holy Spirit, and table fellowship.

Read

Luke 3:1–9:50; Kelly, pages 110–12 and 141–45; EDB articles: "Holy Spirit: Gospels," "Luke," "Luke: Gospel of," and "Meals"; "*L* Passages," #11, and "Material Usually Allotted to *Q*," #12, in the SUPPLEMENTARY READINGS at the back of the student workbook

Rationale for Student Questions

To enable students:

1. To gain a sense of Luke's editorial work in the story of the baptism of Jesus.

2. To recognize how Luke uses the Old Testament to reveal the meaning of the events and words in the life of Jesus.

3. To reflect on Luke's ideal for Christian living and to apply it to their lives.

4. To be aware of the uniqueness of Luke's anointing story.

5. To appreciate the importance of table fellowship in Luke's gospel as a way of revealing Jesus' identity and the role of disciples.

6. To note the continued emphasis on prayer in the Lukan narrative.

Suggested Lecture Topics

- Luke as evangelist.

- Luke's use of his sources: Mark, Q, and L (the special passages unique to his gospel).

- Introduction to redaction criticism.

- Plan of salvation history in Luke-Acts.

- Overview of Luke 3:1–9:50, highlighting those passages/stories that help identify Jesus and the nature of his mission, as well as what it means to be his disciple.

- Lukan themes of fulfillment, forgiveness, prayer, Holy Spirit, and table fellowship as they are developed in Luke 3:1—9:50.

- Connection between Luke's emphasis on the twelve and the twelve tribes of Israel.

SUGGESTED ANSWERS FOR UNIT I.7

1. a. Luke omits the reference to Jesus coming from Nazareth (Mark 1:9).

   Luke adds that "all the people were baptized" and states that Jesus was praying after his baptism (Luke 3:21).

   Luke adds "Holy" to Spirit and says that the Holy Spirit "descended in bodily form" (Luke 3:22).

2. a. Passages in which the evangelist refers to the Old Testament:

   - Luke 4:4 refers to Deuteronomy 8:3.

   - Luke 4:8 refers to Deuteronomy 6:13.

   - Luke 4:10–11 refers to Psalm 91:11–12.

   - Luke 4:12 refers to Deuteronomy 6:16.

   - Luke 4:18–19 refers to Isaiah 61:1–2a; 58:6b.

   - Luke 4:25–26 refers to 1 Kings 17:1–24.

   - Luke 4:27 refers to 2 Kings 5:1–14.

   b. These references help to identify Jesus and his mission in the following ways:

   - Jesus is empowered by the word of God, not by bread (Luke 4:4).

   - Jesus serves God alone (Luke 4:8).

   - Jesus is confident that God is supporting him and his mission (Luke 4:11–12).

   - Jesus was sent by God to rescue all those who are poor, oppressed, and captive (Luke 4:18–19).

   - Jesus provides for others, just as the Old Testament prophets provided for others (Luke 4:25–27).

4. a. Similarities:

   - Both Luke and Mark set the scene in a home where Jesus is a guest at table.

   - In both, an unnamed woman anoints Jesus with ointment from an alabaster flask.

   Differences:

   - In Mark the host is Simon the leper. In Luke the host is Simon the Pharisee.

   - In Luke the woman is a sinner. Mark makes no mention of this.

   - In Mark the woman anoints Jesus' head with the ointment. In Luke she wets his feet with her tears, wipes them with her hair, and anoints them with the oil.

   - In Mark some are angry because of the waste of expensive oil. In Luke the host questions why Jesus would let a sinful woman touch him if he was a prophet.

   - In Mark the anointing takes place just before Jesus' passion and death, and Jesus says that she is anointing him beforehand for his burial. In Luke the anointing takes place earlier in Jesus' ministry and is an expression of love.

   - Luke adds the parable of the two debtors.

- In Mark Jesus praises the woman for anointing him and says that her action will be remembered. In Luke Jesus praises her for her love and her faith, and he forgives her sins.

b. Luke changes the focus of the story from one of preparation for Jesus' passion and death to one of love and forgiveness. In Luke Jesus is seen as a compassionate prophet who has the power to forgive sins.

5. a. Jesus:

- Cares for the outcasts and the sinners (Luke 5:29–30).

- Calls for repentance (Luke 5:31–32).

- Is the bridegroom who inaugurates the new age (Luke 5:34–39).

b. Those whom Jesus calls are to leave everything and follow him (Luke 5:27).

6. Prayer

Reference in Luke	Who Prays	Content
3:21	Jesus	Not given
5:12	Leper	Asks to be made clean
5:16	Jesus	Not given
5:33	John's disciples	Not given
6:12	Jesus	Not given
6:28	Teaching of Jesus	For those who abuse you
7:7	Centurion	Begs for healing for his servant
8:41	Jairus	Begs for healing for his daughter
9:16	Jesus	Blesses the loaves
9:18	Jesus	Not given
9:38	A father	Begs for healing for his son

I.8
Luke 9:51—19:27

Assignment Objectives

To enable students:

1. To recognize the importance of the journey in Luke's gospel.

2. To identify the Lukan themes of prayer, right use of wealth, forgiveness, and reconciliation and to apply what is learned to contemporary life situations.

3. To distinguish Luke's version of the Lord's Prayer from that of Matthew.

4. To note the special Lukan material that has been grouped in the journey section (Luke 9:51—19:27) of this gospel.

5. To understand Luke's use of parables as illustrative or example stories.

6. To recognize how the placement of parables in a certain context helps determine their meaning.

Read

Luke 9:51—19:27; Kelly, pages 145–48; EDB articles: "Father," "Lord's Prayer," "Samaritans," and "Sin: New Testament"

Rationale for Student Questions

To enable students:

1. To recognize the importance of love in Luke's understanding of Christian living.

2. To distinguish between and reflect upon the versions of the Lord's Prayer in Matthew and Luke.

3. To understand the Lukan use of parables and to apply the message of the parables to their lives.

4. To focus on the Lukan theme of right use of wealth.

5. To explore the uniquely Lukan passages in the journey section and to reflect on the relevance of these passages to their lives.

6. To reinforce their awareness of the importance of prayer as a theme in Luke's gospel.

Suggested Lecture Topics

- Journey narrative; its nature and purpose.

- Importance of Jerusalem as the immediate goal of the journey.

- Special Lukan material (*L* passages) found in the journey section (Luke 9:51—19:27).

- Luke's use of parables as example stories to illustrate the way of Christian discipleship.

- Further development of Lukan themes in the journey section.

- Jesus in relation to the poor, the outcasts, and non-Jews.

- Social justice and Christian behavior in Luke.

- Luke's emphasis on the proper use of wealth.

SUGGESTED ANSWERS FOR UNIT I.8

1. Love for God is primary and unlimited. We are to love God with our whole being. Our love for our neighbor is to match our love of self.

    The Good Samaritan parable adds to the understanding of love of neighbor. Jesus broadens the concept of neighbor from the limited understanding of neighbor as a fellow covenant member to an understanding that includes the outsider and perhaps even the enemy. What is important is not so much who meets the criterion of neighbor, and so can be loved by me, as much as the fact that I must be neighbor to others in the first place, as the Samaritan was neighbor.

    The story of Mary and Martha emphasizes the necessity of listening to the Lord in love as well as acting

2. a. In both Matthew and Luke, the prayer appears to be the prayer of the community. In Luke a disciple asks, "Lord, teach *us* to pray..." (Luke 11:1). In Matthew the prayer begins with, "*Our* Father" (Matt 6:9). The petitions in both gospels use *us* and *our*, not *me* and *mine* (Luke 11:3-4; Matt 6:11-13). It is difficult to argue against the notion that this prayer is primarily a community prayer.

    b. According to the prayer, we are to pray for the coming of the kingdom (Luke 11:2b; Matt 6:10), our daily sustenance (Luke 11:3; Matt 6:11), God's forgiveness (Luke 11:4a; Matt 6:12), and being spared from temptation (Luke 11:4b; Matt 6:13).

    c. Significant differences:

       • Matthew begins the prayer with "Our Father" (Matt 6:9). Luke does not include the "our" (Luke 11:2).

       • Luke's version of the prayer is shorter. He does not include "Thy will be done on earth as it is in heaven" (Matt 6:10b) or the petition "deliver us from evil" (Matt 6:13b).

       • Luke's version asks for forgiveness of sins (Luke 11:4a) while Matthew's version asks for forgiveness of debts (Matt 6:12).

3. a. Each parable demonstrates the boundless compassion of God for human beings in their weakness and failure. There is joy over one who is found (Luke 10:7, 10, and 32). Also, note the search necessary for the finding of the lost (Luke 15:4, 8). The third parable, the Prodigal Son, shows God's readiness to welcome back and forgive the one who was lost.

    b. These parables challenge us to open our own hearts. God's compassionate and forgiving response to the lost is a model for us to follow. These parables call us to be welcoming, loving, and merciful members of the community.

4. These chapters challenge us to use our wealth wisely and in the service of others, especially the poor (Luke 10:29-37; 11:42; 12:33-34; 14:12-14; 16:19-31; 18:22-25; 19:8). We are called to be good stewards of our gifts (Luke 19:11-27). We are also warned against greed and putting possessions in the place of God (Luke 12:15-21, 34; 16:10-13).

6. Prayer

Reference in Luke	Who Prays	Content
10:21	Jesus	Thanks the Father for revelation to the disciples
11:1	Jesus	Not given
11:2–4	Jesus	Lord's Prayer
13:13	Crippled woman	Glorifies God
13:17	Crowd	Rejoices at all the deeds done by Jesus
17:13	Ten lepers	Ask for healing
17:15–16	Samaritan leper	Thanksgiving for being healed
18:38–41	Blind beggar	Asks for mercy and sight
18:43	Blind beggar	Glorifies and praises God for his sight

*The ideal condition would be, I admit,
that people should be right by instinct,
but since we are likely to go astray,
the reasonable thing is to learn
from those who can teach.*
—Sophocles, Antigone, 720

I.9
Luke 19:28—24:53

Assignment Objectives

To enable students:

1. To recognize the uniqueness of Luke's passion narrative, noticing the changes in emphasis from the tradition of Mark.

2. To see how Luke's passion and resurrection narratives have been shaped to express the major themes of his gospel, in particular his portrait of Jesus and his understanding of genuine discipleship.

3. To recognize how Luke's resurrection narrative does or does not lead into Acts of the Apostles.

Read

Luke 19:28–24:53; Kelly, pages 149–56; EDB articles: "Ascension: Jesus" and "Resurrection"

Rationale for Student Questions

To enable students:

1. To examine the institution narratives in Luke and Mark and to make connections with the eucharistic liturgy.
2. To note how Luke's editing of the text presents a particular view of who Jesus is.
3. To recognize how insights from Luke's resurrection narrative can be applied to their lives.
4. To distinguish between the portraits of Jesus found in Luke and in Mark.
5. To note how Jesus continues his mission of healing, forgiveness, and reconciliation even during his passion and after his resurrection.
6. To appreciate the continued importance of prayer in the Gospel of Luke.

Suggested Lecture Topics

- Uniquely Lukan elements in the passion/resurrection narratives; reinforcing the idea of Luke as a real author and reexamining his theological purpose in shaping his gospel.

- Continued development of major Lukan themes in the passion and resurrection narratives.

- Luke's interpretation of the meaning of Jesus' death:
  - As the way to new life with the Father
  - As a witness to Jesus' prophetic message and life
  - As a test of perseverance in following God's way

- Significance of the passion and resurrection narratives in Catholic liturgy and prayer.

SUGGESTED ANSWERS FOR UNIT I.9

1. a. Similarities:

    • In both versions Jesus takes the bread, breaks it, and gives it to his disciples, saying, "This is my body" (Luke 22:19; Mark 14:11).

    • He also takes the cup and refers to it as "my blood" (Luke 22:20–21; Mark 14:23–24).

    Differences:

    • Luke prefaces the institution narrative with a statement by Jesus about desiring to eat the Passover with the disciples before he suffers (Luke 22:15–16). This statement is not found in Mark.

    • Luke has Jesus take a cup prior to taking the bread, give thanks, and tell the disciples to divide it among themselves (Luke 22:17).

    • Luke places Jesus' statement about not drinking from the fruit of the vine before the institution rather than after it as Mark does (Luke 22:18; Mark 14:25).

    • Luke says that Jesus gave thanks over the bread (Luke 22:19) and Mark says he blessed it (Mark 14:22).

    • Luke adds "which is given for you. Do this in remembrance of me" after "This is my body" (Luke 22:19b).

    • Mark says that Jesus gave thanks over the cup and "they all drank of it" (Mark 14:23).

    • Note that Luke refers to two cups. Jesus takes the second cup and says, "This cup which is poured out for you is the new covenant in my blood" (Luke 22:20b) while in Mark he says, "This is my blood of the covenant which is poured out for many" (Mark 14:24).

2. In Luke 23:39–43, Jesus:

    • Is the one in whom and through whom forgiveness and salvation come.

    • Does not correct the criminal's statement, and so is described not only as being innocent, but also as being one who possesses unique authority and power.

    • Comes to forgive and save those who are lost.

3. We can recognize the presence of the Risen Lord in the scriptures (Luke 24:25–27, 32), in the breaking of the bread (Luke 24:30–31, 35), and in the mysterious strangers we meet on our life journey (Luke 24:15–16).

4. a.

Jesus in Mark's Passion Story	Jesus in Luke's Passion Story
In Mark, Jesus:	In Luke, Jesus:
Is "distressed and agitated" (Mark 14:33b). Is "deeply grieved, even to death" (Mark 14:34).	Is not described as being "distressed and agitated" or as being "deeply grieved, even to death."
Throws himself on the ground (Mark 14:35).	Kneels down and prays (Luke 22:41).
Faces his passion alone. Takes only three disciples with him; goes off to pray alone; and finds the disciples sleeping three times (Mark 14:32b–33a, 37–42). He is abandoned by all (Mark 14:50–52).	Appears to be less isolated than in Mark. Is followed by his disciples to the place of prayer; and finds the disciples sleeping only once (Luke 22:39b, 45–46). Is not described as being abandoned by all.
Cries out from the cross, "My God, my God, why have you forsaken me?" (Mark 15:34).	Cries out from the cross, "Father, into your hands I commend my spirit" (Luke 23:46).
Has only the women look on from a distance as he dies on the cross (Mark 15:40).	Has all of his acquaintances looking on from a distance as he dies on the cross (Luke 23:49).
	Is a man of compassion, who heals the high priest's slave (Luke 22:51), brings about reconciliation between Herod and Pilate (Luke 23:12), comforts the women he meets on the way to the cross (Luke 23:27–28), forgives those who crucify him (Luke 23:34), and promises salvation to the repentant criminal (Luke 23:43).
Is called "God's son," after he dies, by a centurion (Mark 14:39).	Is proclaimed innocent three times by Pilate (Luke 23:4, 14–15, 22), by the criminal crucified with him (Luke 23:41), and (after he dies) by a centurion (Luke 23:47).

5. Some examples of healing, forgiveness and reconciliation:

- Jesus heals the ear of the high priest's slave (Luke 22:51).

- Herod and Pilate become friends after Pilate sends Jesus to Herod (Luke 23:12).

- Jesus forgives those who are crucifying him (Luke 23:34a).

- Jesus promises the criminal that he will be with him in Paradise (Luke 23:43).

- Jesus says, "repentance and forgiveness of sins is to be proclaimed in his name to all nations, beginning from Jerusalem" (Luke 24:47).

6. Prayer

Reference in Luke	Who Prays	Content
19:37–38	Multitude of disciples	Praise God for the deeds of power they had seen
22:17	Jesus	Gives thanks over the cup
22:19	Jesus	Gives thanks over the bread
22:32	Jesus	That Peter's faith would not fail and that he would strengthen the brothers
22:41	Jesus	Asks that the cup be removed, but also that the Father's will be done
23:42	Criminal	Asks Jesus to remember him
23:46	Jesus	Commends his spirit into the Father's hand
23:47	Centurion	Glorifies God
23:48	Crowd	Beat their breasts
24:30	Jesus	Blesses the bread
24:51	Jesus	Blesses the disciples
24:52	The disciples	Worship Jesus and bless God in the temple

I.10
Unit One Review

Students will be responsible for:

1. A memory verse from either Mark's gospel or Luke's gospel, indicating the translation used and citing reference.

2. The information included in the following SUPPLEMENTARY READINGS at the back of the student workbook:
   - #2. "The Three Stages of the Composition of the Gospels (Vatican II)"
   - #3. "The Synoptic Gospels and Their Sources"
   - #5. "The Gospel According to Mark: Overview"
   - #7. "Self-Quiz on Mark's Gospel"
   - #8. "Luke-Acts: Overview"
   - #14. "Self-Quiz on Luke's Gospel"

3. The location of the following places and areas on a map of the Holy Land:

Bethany	Judea
Bethlehem	Nain
Bethsaida	Nazareth
Caesarea Philippi	Phoenicia
Capernaum	Samaria
Dead Sea	Sea of Galilee
Decapolis	Sidon
Galilee	Syria
Gerasa	Tyre
Jericho	

Suggested Lecture Topics

– Review the three stages of gospel composition, definition of a gospel, and role of the evangelist as an author.

– Emphasize that the gospels are catechetical documents. The evangelists' goal is to form the faith and behavior of their communities.

– Review the synoptic problem and the nature and relevance of the Q source.

– Review the basic facts for Mark and Luke: date of composition, audience, historical/social/religious situation of the community, purpose for writing the gospel, structure of the gospel, portrait of Jesus, portrait of Christian discipleship, and major themes.

– Review the geography of the Holy Land.

1. List and explain the three stages in the formation of the gospels.

2. Briefly explain the meaning of the following terms:

   a. Synoptic Gospels

   b. Q Source

3. How would you describe Mark's purpose for writing his gospel?

4. How would you characterize the portrait of Jesus in Mark's gospel?

5. How would you characterize the portrait of Christian discipleship in Mark's gospel?

6. Briefly explain what you consider to be the most important theme in Mark's gospel.

7. How would you describe Luke's purpose for writing his gospel?

8. How would you characterize the portrait of Jesus in Luke's gospel?

9. How would you characterize the portrait of Christian discipleship in Luke's gospel?

10. Briefly explain what you consider to be the most important theme in Luke's gospel.

11. What is the most significant thing you have learned during your study of Mark and Luke?

12. Write your memory verse from Mark or Luke. Include reference and translation used.

MAP

I. Write the number of each of the following places next to the appropriate dot on the map:

1. Bethlehem

2. Caesarea Philippi

3. Capernaum

4. Gerasa

5. Jericho

6. Nazareth

II. Indicate on the map where the following are located:

Dead Sea

Decapolis

Galilee

Judea

Phoenicia

Samaria

Sea of Galilee

Syria

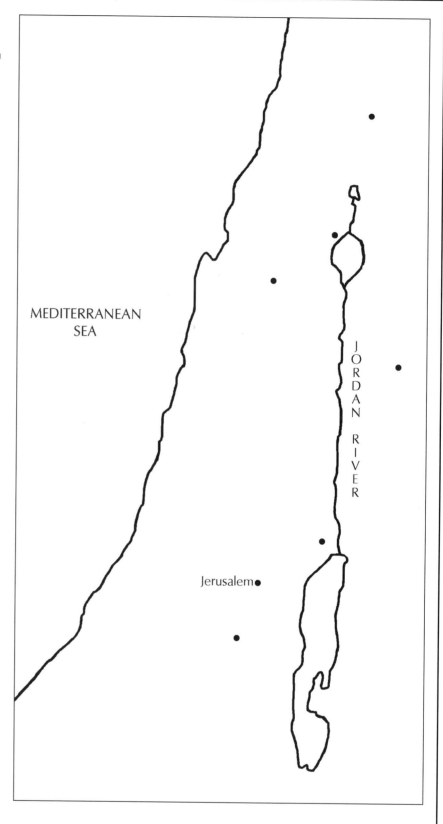

MEDITERRANEAN
SEA

JORDAN RIVER

Jerusalem

34

ANSWERS TO YEAR TWO–UNIT ONE TEST

1. Stage One: The actual events of Jesus' life and the actual words he preached.

   Stage Two: Oral preaching and teaching by the apostles adapted for their listeners, after the ascension of Jesus.

   Stage Three: Written gospels by the evangelists adapted for their communities.

2. a. Synoptic gospels are the gospels of Mark, Matthew, and Luke, which can be "viewed together" because they follow the same outline of the story of Jesus, which cannot be said for John.
   b. Q source is a hypothetical source used to explain the existence of common material (mostly sayings of Jesus) in Matthew and Luke, not found in Mark.

3. Mark's gospel was written in order to proclaim the Christian message in a way that would re-orient the community's understanding of Jesus' suffering and death and the demands of their own discipleship in a time of suffering and distress.

4. Mark's primary characterization of Jesus is that he is the Christ and Son of God. He is the Suffering Son of Man who gives up his life for the people. Other characterizations are possible.

5. Mark characterizes the Christian disciple as one who undergoes a conversion and comes to faith in Jesus Christ. The Christian disciple gives a wholehearted response to Christ's call to follow him. The Christian disciple also denies self, gives one's life for others, and takes up one's cross.

6. Possibilities include: understanding/misunderstanding the identity of Jesus and what it means to be his disciple; unity in community through the Eucharist; combat between good and evil; insiders/outsiders (those hear the word of God and do the will of God contrasted with those who don't hear and believe); and miracles as signs of Jesus' authority and of his ushering in the kingdom of God. There are other possibilities.

7. Luke's gospel was written in order to provide an authoritative account of the history of salvation as revealed and fulfilled in the life and ministry of Jesus and continued in the life and ministry of the Christian Church.

8. Luke's primary characterization of Jesus is that he is the Messiah and Lord. He is the saving (healing) prophet who demonstrates the mercy of God and saves us from our sins.

9. Luke characterizes the Christian disciple as one who seeks God's mercy and forgiveness and responds wholeheartedly to God's call. The Christian disciple hears the word of God and acts on it through prayer, seeking the empowerment of the Holy Spirit to be a Spirit-filled witness, and reaching out to seek and save the lost.

10. Possibilities include: prayer; universal salvation; table fellowship; right use of wealth; prayer and praise of God; the role of the Holy Spirit; the role of women; and Christian life as a journey with Jesus the Lord. There are other possibilities.

11. Many possibilities. This gives you, the teacher, a chance to discover what in this unit has been most significant for your students.

12. Any passage from Mark or Luke. Reference and translation used must be included.

MAP

I. Reading from north to south:

    2. Caesarea Philippi

    3. Capernaum

    6. Nazareth

    4. Gerasa

    5. Jericho

    1. Bethlehem

II. The areas in north-to-south order are:

    Syria

    Phoenicia (along the coast of the Mediterranean Sea)

    Galilee

    Samaria (west of Jordan River)

    Decapolis (east of Jordan River)

    Judea

        (Consult the Hammond Atlas for exact locations)

    The sea in the north is the Sea of Galilee.

    The sea in the south is the Dead Sea.

UNIT II
Jesus: A Pauline View

Objectives

To enable students:

1. To explain the chronology, geography, and social and cultural environment of early Christianity.

2. To recognize the Christian message through an investigation of the structure, themes, and theology of Acts of the Apostles and Paul's letters.

3. To use Acts of the Apostles and Paul's letters for personal and communal prayer.

Textbooks   **Primary Text:** The Bible. Use a good translation with scholarly notes.

Other Texts: For helpful background and handy reference we recommend:
Eerdmans *Dictionary of the Bible* (cited as EDB)
Hammond's *Atlas of the Bible Lands* (cited as Hammond Atlas)
Joseph Kelly, *An Introduction to the New Testament for Catholics* (cited as Kelly)

Assignments   Each lesson is to be studied by the students in preparation for their group discussion. For each biblical passage, students study the biblical text and footnotes for that particular passage, do other assigned readings, and answer the written work *on a separate page*.

   II.1   ACTS OF THE APOSTLES 1–12

   II.2   ACTS OF THE APOSTLES 13–28

   II.3   1 and 2 THESSALONIANS; PHILIPPIANS

   II.4   1 CORINTHIANS

   II.5   2 CORINTHIANS

   II.6   GALATIANS

   II.7   ROMANS 1–4

   II.8   ROMANS 5–16

   II.9   COLOSSIANS; EPHESIANS; PHILEMON

   II.10 UNIT TWO REVIEW

   UNIT TWO TEST

II.1
Acts of the Apostles 1–12

Assignment Objectives

To enable students:

1. To explain why Luke wrote Acts of the Apostles.

2. To recognize the Gospel of Luke and the Acts of the Apostles as one integrated work.

3. To describe the early church's outreach to and inclusion of Gentiles.

4. To identify the major themes of Acts of the Apostles, including (a) the growth and development of the early church, (b) the movement to include the Gentiles in the early church, and (c) the role of Peter in the early church.

5. To describe the role and theology of the Holy Spirit from Luke's perspective.

6. To locate Samaria, Damascus, Antioch in Syria, Lydda, Joppa, Caesarea (different from Caesarea Philippi), Phoenicia, Cyprus and Cilicia on a map.

Read

Acts 1–12; Kelly, pages 179–93; EDB articles: "Acts of the Apostles," "Pentecost," and "Stephen"; "Luke-Acts: Overview," #8 in the SUPPLEMENTARY READINGS at the back of the student workbook

Rationale for Student Questions

To enable students:

1. To recognize the two versions of the ascension of Jesus and learn that one forms the basis of the church's liturgical calendar.

2. To see how Luke uses the Old Testament to illuminate the meaning of events.

3. To discover Luke's theology of church (a rather idealized view, but note that suffering, persecution, and internal problems are also present).

4. To explore the traditional origin and meaning of the diaconate.

5. To discover the interconnection of Luke-Acts and to see Jesus as the model for Christian ministry and death.

6. To trace Luke's theology of God in action through the Holy Spirit.

Suggested Lecture Topics

– Acts of the Apostles as a continuation of message and themes begun in the Gospel of Luke.

– Overview of structure and principal themes in Acts of the Apostles.

– Overall theme/movement of the entire book as a development of Acts 1:8.

– Meaning of history for first-century people as not simply what happened but an explanation of events that always included the power of God as an active force in what happened.

– Jesus in Luke's gospel as the model for the characterization of the apostles and consequently of all disciples (note the pattern of empowerment by the Holy Spirit, witness in preaching and miracles, suffering).

– The Christian Church as a community of witness and service.

– Growth of the church from *followers of the way* to *Christians.*

– Connection between the Spirit of God in the Lukan story and the same Spirit of God that animates the church today.

– Deacons' role today related to that of the men chosen in Acts of the Apostles 6:1–6.

SUGGESTED ANSWERS FOR UNIT II.1

1. a. Luke 24 indicates that Jesus ascended on Easter Sunday evening (Luke 24:1, 13, 50, 51). Acts of the Apostles 1 says that Jesus continued to appear to the apostles throughout a period of forty days (Acts 1:3) before he ascended (once and for all?) into heaven (Acts 1:9). There are additional possibilities.

   b. The story in Acts of the Apostles guides the liturgical calendar of the church today as we celebrate "Ascension Thursday" forty days after Easter Sunday.

2. a. Luke may be influenced by the following Old Testament images:

   • They all stood at the bottom of the mountain (Exodus 19:17; Acts 2:1)

   • Wind of God (Gen 1:2; Acts 2:2)

   • The LORD had descended in the form of fire (Exod 19:18; Acts 2:3)

   • Multiplicity of languages (Gen 11:1–11; Acts 2:6)

   b. Luke uses theophany imagery from the Old Testament to show that the Spirit of God was present at Pentecost to embolden the disciples. The Tower of Babel incident (Gen 11:1–11) describes humanity relying on itself and attempting to make a name for itself in order to achieve unity and solidarity. The result is punishment (confusion of languages), which leads to a scattering of the people. In the Pentecost event (Acts 2:1–6), the disciples, when submitting to the power of the Holy Spirit, achieve unity and oneness as symbolized in universal understanding. In a sense, Pentecost reverses Babel by speaking of human unity and solidarity through the power of God's initiative, not human resources.

3. a. Luke stresses that the Christian community is characterized by devotion to the apostles' teaching, fellowship, breaking of the bread, and prayer (Acts 2:42). Community members enjoyed unity of heart and mind (Acts 4:32); they shared their possessions and property in community life through the guidance of the apostles (Acts 4:32, 34–36), witnessed to the resurrection (Acts 4:33) despite the persecution of the Jewish leaders and Sanhedrin (Acts 4:1–31), praised God (Acts 4:21) and prayed as a response to their suffering for Christ's sake (Acts 4:23–31).

   b. These characteristics relate to such Lukan themes as right use of wealth/sharing (Acts 4:36–37; 5:1–11), breaking of the bread (Luke 24; Acts 2:46), the hostility of the Jewish leaders (Acts 4:1–22; 5:17), and the importance of prayer (Acts 3:1).

4. a. Some Hellenist widows were being overlooked in the daily distribution of the bread. The apostles wanted to spend their time in prayer and service to the word, so they appointed seven individuals to serve at table (Acts 6:1-6).

   b. The qualifications for the seven included their being men of good standing, who were filled with the Spirit and with wisdom.

5. Some parallels between the death of Jesus and the death of Stephen:

- False witnesses and a blasphemy charge (Acts 6:11, 13) are similar to accusations against Jesus that are found to be without merit (Luke 23:2–4).

- Hostile crowd, arrest, brought before the authorities (Acts 6:12; Luke 22:54, 63, 66–67)

- Mention of Son of Man in power (Acts 7:55–56; Luke 22:69)

- Trial ends with desire for execution (Acts 7:57–58; Luke 23:23)

- Commending of spirit at time of death (Acts 7:59; Luke 23:46)

- Forgiving/asking God to forgive executioners (Acts 7:60; Luke 23:34)

6. Possibilities include:

- The Pentecost experience and Peter's speech (Acts 2)

- Peter and community witness boldly (Acts 4:8, 31)

- The Holy Spirit guides the deacon Philip in his ministry (Acts 8:39)

- The church has peace and grows through the Holy Spirit (Acts 9:31)

- The Holy Spirit helps Peter decide to turn to the Gentiles (Acts 10:19, 44–47; 11:12, 15)

II.2
Acts of the Apostles 13–28

Assignment Objectives

To enable students:

1. To begin to appreciate the person and work of Paul.

2. To see Paul as representative of the church's turn to the Gentile nations.

3. To begin to distinguish Luke's portrait of Paul from the portrait found in Paul's letters.

4. To recognize how Luke continues the theological themes from his gospel in Acts of the Apostles.

5. To note the implications for the church of the shift from Judaism to the Hellenistic Gentile world.

6. To locate Cyprus, Antioch in Pisidia, Galatia, Macedonia, Athens, Corinth, Crete, Malta, and Rome on a map.

Read

Acts 13–28; Kelly, pages 31–39 and 193–200; "Chronology of Paul's Life," #15 in the SUPPLEMENTARY READINGS at the back of the student workbook

Rationale for Student Questions

To enable students:

1. To discover the Lukan view of Paul: prominent here is Luke's theology of mission—first to Jews (rejection), then to Gentiles (acceptance).

2. To discover Paul's approach to the Gentiles, a people who do not know the Old Testament.

3. To relate Luke's message of ministry (as exemplified in Paul) to today.

4. To recognize each author's purpose in relating the story of the Council in Jerusalem by differentiating Luke's version in Acts of the Apostles from that found in Paul's letter to the Galatians.

5. To respond creatively to the biblical text.

Suggested Lecture Topics

- Introduction to Paul (who he is, his background, what gifts he brought to the task for which God called him).

- Paul and the growth of the early church.

- Paul's journeys.

- Compare and contrast Luke's view of Paul with Paul's own view of himself.

- Major Lukan themes that are present in Acts of the Apostles 13–28.

- How Luke's gospel and Acts of the Apostles complement one another.

SUGGESTED ANSWERS FOR UNIT II.2

1. The typical pattern of Paul's missionary activity in Acts 13 would look something like this:

   - Paul begins preaching in a synagogue to Jews and Gentile God-fearers (Acts 13:14, 16–41)

   - Rejection by most Jews (Acts 13:45, 50)

   - Paul turns to the Gentiles, many of whom accept the message (Acts 13:46–48)

   - Birth of a new community (Acts 13:48–49)

   - Persecution arising out of rejection by the Jews (Acts 13:45, 50)

   - Departure to another town, where the pattern begins again (Acts 13:51)

2. a. Paul's description of God and God's past relationship with the Gentiles (based on Acts 14:15–17; 17:22–31) would include the following points:

   - God is identified as a living God, as opposed to dead idols fashioned by human hands (Acts 14:15; 17:29).

   - God causes rain and growth of crops; he gives food and makes people happy (Acts 14:17).

   - God is the one whom the Athenians recognize as the "Unknown God" (Acts 17:23).

   - God is creator of the world, who does not dwell in anything made by human hands (Acts 17:24).

   - In the past, God let the nations (Gentiles) go their own way, yet was present to them by acting on their behalf in the natural world (Acts 14:15–17).

   b. Now God demands repentance before the day of judgment (Acts 17:30–31).

4. a. Some differences between the two accounts of the Council in Jerusalem:

   - Galatians says this is Paul's second visit to Jerusalem, but in Acts of the Apostles it is his third. In Galatians there is no mention of a famine visit (cf. Acts 11:28–30).

   - In Galatians, Paul takes Titus, an uncircumcised Gentile, with him (Gal 2:1). In Acts of the Apostles there is no mention of Titus (cf. Acts 15).

   - In Galatians, Paul goes up to Jerusalem because of a revelation (Gal 2:2). In Acts of the Apostles, he goes up because there is strife regarding the need for circumcision in order to be saved (Acts 15:2).

   - In Galatians, there is only one issue resulting in no need for the circumcision of Gentiles. Nothing is added to Paul's assertion (Gal 2). In Acts of the Apostles, the issues are circumcision and the Mosaic Law (Acts 15:3–12).

   - Paul knows nothing about the letter to the Gentiles (Acts 15:20, 30b). In fact, Paul needs to be told about the letter later by James (cf. Acts 21:25). There is no apostolic decree in Galatians. If there were we wouldn't have the Antioch incident (cf. Gal 2:11–14). In Galatians, Paul says, "They asked only one thing, that we remember the poor" (Gal 2:10).

II.3
1 and 2 Thessalonians; Philippians

Assignment Objectives

To enable students:

1. To better understand Paul's words, his world, and his use of letter writing.

2. To note that Paul's letters are responses to pastoral concerns in various communities at that time.

3. To recognize that Paul uses many images to convey his understanding of the person and saving work of Jesus Christ.

4. To identify the historical, social, and religious situations of the Thessalonian and Philippian communities that prompted Paul's response.

5. To acknowledge that there are questions regarding the authorship of some Pauline letters.

6. To locate Thessalonica, Achaia, and Philippi on a map.

Read

1 and 2 Thessalonians; Philippians; Kelly, pages 40–42, 49–53, and 201–3; EDB articles: "Eschatology: Paul," "Kenosis," and "Parousia"; "Raptured or Not?" #17, and "The Letters of Paul: Overview—Paul, 1 Thessalonians, 2 Thessalonians, Philippians," #18, in the SUPPLE-MENTARY READINGS at the back of the student workbook

Rationale for Student Questions

To enable students:

1. To discover the situation of the Thessalonian community and its problems.

2. To recognize the importance of the imminent return of Jesus (the *parousia*) in the early church.

3. To clarify the Catholic perspective on the question of the Rapture.

4. To discover how Paul expresses his understanding of Jesus (Christology) by using a Christian hymn.

5. To relate scripture to personal life and spiritual growth.

6. To relate the *parousia* to today.

Suggested Lecture Topics

– The letter as a unique way of proclaiming the Christian message.

– Background information on the literary genre of letter in the Hellenistic world: the standard form of a letter, how letters were written, reasons for Paul's use of letters, etc.

– Paul as a pastoral theologian rather than a systematic theologian.

– Paul's method of relating particular problems to the more general teachings of the Christian message.

– Introduction to the communities of Thessalonica and Philippi during Paul's time (i.e., where they are, who they are, what is happening that occasions Paul's letters to them).

– The genre or type of literature controls the way we must try to interpret its meaning. Since Paul's letters are the first experience of the students so far with biblical writing that is not narrative, students should focus on:
   • Rhetorical or persuasive strategies Paul uses to make his positions clear and forceful
   • Correlation between Paul's solutions and the problems experienced by his communities

SUGGESTED ANSWERS FOR UNIT II.3

1. Some things we learn about the early Christian community from I Thessalonians 1 include the following:

- Faith, hope, and love characterized the Christian community then, as it does today (1 Thess 1:3).

- Although the word *trinity* is not used anywhere in the Bible to describe God, nevertheless it is clear from 1 Thessalonians 1:1–10 that Paul distinguishes God the Father (1 Thess 1:1, 3, 10), Jesus as God's Son and Lord (1 Thess 1:1, 3, 6, 10) and the Holy Spirit (1 Thess 1:5, 6).

- The Christian community is engaged in missionary/conversion activity (1 Thess 1:5–9).

- The community attributes the success of missionary activity to God (Holy Spirit) using preachers and missionaries as instruments (1 Thess 1:5). If the Holy Spirit is allowed to work and the faith is accepted and lived out by the new community, the good news spreads of its own to neighboring communities, demonstrating the power of the word of God and the Spirit (1 Thess 1:6–10).

- As a converted community, it has been chosen by God and called from a previous form of life and belief (from idol-worship of dead and false gods, 1 Thess 1:4, 9) to a continually growing relationship with a powerful God who is living and true, and who is Savior (1 Thess 1:3, 9–10).

- The community's new lifestyle incurs wrath and persecution (1 Thess 1:6).

- Prayer is important for communities new in the faith (1 Thess 1:2).

2. Significant similarities and differences:

Important Issues Addressed	1 Thessalonians 5:1–12	2 Thessalonians 2:1–12
Focus of passage	The *parousia*	The *parousia*
When the *parousia* will occur	The *parousia* is near, but the exact time is uncertain.	Belief that the *parousia* is already present is a false notion. Use of an apocalyptic scenario to speak of certain signs that must precede Christ's second coming and victory.
Consequences for Christians	Christians should behave in a certain way in the interim. For those unprepared, the *parousia* is a time to be feared; but for those prepared, it is a time of consolation.	Assurance of Christ's victory produces consolation for the faithful and defeat and fear for apostates.
Question concerning those already dead at the time of the *parousia*	Those already dead at the time of the *parousia* are no better or worse off than those alive.	Not addressed

3. a. The trumpet of God, the voice of the angel, the Lord coming down from heaven, the dead will rise (1 Thess 4:16), living will be caught up in the clouds, meeting the Lord in the air (1 Thess 4:17).

  b. "…we will be with the Lord forever" (1 Thess 4:17).

4. a. i. The three major stages are:

   • The preexistence of Christ (Phil 2:6–7a).

   • The earthly existence of Christ (Phil 2:7b–8).

   • The exaltation of Christ (Phil 2:9–11).

  ii. He becomes truly human (Phil 2:7b) and is totally obedient, even to death on the cross (Phil 2:8).

  iii. Jesus Christ has been highly exalted and given the name above all other names—Lord.

What remains for us is to take Paul's principles and apply them to our situation today. What remains for us is to be a community open to the Spirit and not millions of individuals each going his own way. What remains for us is to have the courage to face the truth. What remains for us is to follow the way of Jesus as taught by Paul.

—Emil A. Wcela, Paul the Pastor

II.4
1 Corinthians

To enable students:

1. To identify the geography and social situation of the Corinthian community and the problems for which this letter offers solutions.

2. To grasp Paul's exhortation to Christ-centered behavior.

3. To recognize Pauline themes of love, wisdom, Eucharist, eschatology, ecclesiology, and the gifts of the Spirit.

4. To articulate Paul's message in 1 Corinthians.

5. To locate Corinth and Ephesus on a map.

Read   1 Corinthians; Kelly, pages 54–63; EDB articles: "Body," "Body of Christ," "Corinth," "Corinthians, First Letter to the," and "Resurrection: New Testament"; "The Letters of Paul: Overview—1 Corinthians," #18, and "House Churches and the Eucharist," #19, in the SUPPLEMENTARY READINGS at the back of the student workbook

Rationale for Student Questions

To enable students:

1. To appreciate Paul's Christian way of solving community problems and to apply Paul's insights to the church today.

2. To become familiar with Paul's method of solving a problem and to see the relationship between the scripture text and the modern world.

3. To recognize the similarities and differences between Paul's institution narrative, the institution narratives in the synoptic gospels, and our own liturgy today. To explore Paul's theology of the eucharistic meal.

4. To analyze closely Paul's teaching on the charismatic gifts.

5. To explore Paul's concept of resurrection.

Suggested Lecture Topics

- Geography of Corinth.

- The Corinthian community and its problems.

- Structure and major themes of 1 Corinthians.

- Paul's understanding of charismatic gifts and their relevance today.

- Eucharist in the early church.

- 1 Corinthians 15 as a reflection of early church's belief (a creed).

- Jewish and Hellenistic understandings of the role of the body, and how these understandings would result in different views of what resurrection will be like.

  • Greeks wanted the soul alone to escape the body rather than to be reunited with it after death.

  • Jews could not think of being human without having some kind of body.

SUGGESTED ANSWERS FOR UNIT II.4

1. a. Divisions within the community stem from groups claiming a special connection with one or another of the Christian leaders (1 Cor 1:12–13; 3:4). Some may claim to be spiritual. The worldly wisdom involved in setting human standards of special distinction may indicate the spiritual immaturity of the Corinthians who are inclined to accept this type of wisdom rather than the wisdom of the cross.

   b. Unity can be achieved primarily by a mature mindset resembling the self-sacrificing mindset of Christ (the cross). True wisdom consists in the sovereignty of Christ in all things. While Paul's advice is not very specific, he exhorts the people to remember how he behaved when he was with them and to act in a similar fashion—living the wisdom of the cross.

3. a. Luke's institution account is closest to the one in 1 Corinthians. Both contain the following phrases not found in Mark and Matthew:

   - [Jesus] took bread *and when he had given thanks* (Luke 22:19a; 1 Cor 11:24a).

   - This is my body *which is* [given] *for you. Do this in remembrance of me* (Luke 22:19b; 1 Cor 11:24b).

   - *The cup after supper* (Luke 22:20a; 1 Cor 11:25a).

   - *The new covenant in my blood* (Luke 22:20b; 1 Cor 11:25b).

   c. Paul's words are the basis for Memorial Acclamation C: "When we eat this bread and drink this cup, we proclaim your death, Lord Jesus, until you come in glory."

4. a. The main criterion for evaluating any spiritual gift is love, as it is described in 1 Corinthains 13. Love builds up the community and does not divide it. According to 1 Corinthians 12:3, Jesus himself is the criterion. Nothing inspired by the Spirit can be against Jesus.

   b. All parts of the body must work in harmony if the whole is to function properly.

   c. Each body part (spiritual gift) makes a distinct and essential contribution to the life of the entire body. Each part is dependent on the others (1 Cor 12:25–26). Therefore, all gifts are important and necessary as they work together for the good of the whole community.

   d. If "God is Love," then 1 Corinthians 13 is also a description of God.

5. a. Paul cites his own eyewitness testimony and the eyewitness testimony of others.

   b. The first question: "How are the dead raised?"
   Paul's answer: It will happen in an instant (1 Cor 15:51–52).
   The second question: "With what kind of body do they come?
   Paul's answer: "It is raised a spiritual body" (1 Cor 15:44) because "flesh and blood cannot inherit the kingdom of God" (1 Cor 15:50).

II.5
2 Corinthians

Assignment Objectives

To enable students:

1. To identify the major themes of 2 Corinthians.

2. To detect Paul's growth in self-knowledge.

3. To describe Paul's view of what it means to be an apostle, his own experience of being an apostle, and the importance of his role as an apostle in the community.

4. To continue to see how Paul relates his theology to practical problems.

5. To become more familiar with the complexity of the relationship of Paul and the Corinthian community and the problems addressed in 2 Corinthians.

6. To recognize the significance of community for the early church.

7. To locate the Roman provinces of Troas, Macedonia, and Asia on a map.

Read

2 Corinthians; Kelly, pages 63–69; EDB articles: "Apostle" and "Corinthians, Second Letter to the"; "The Letters of Paul: Overview—2 Corinthians," #18, and "You Are the Body of Christ," #20, in the SUPPLEMENTARY READINGS at the back of the student workbook

Rationale for Student Questions

To enable students:

1. To discover Paul's theology of ministry.

2. To clarify Paul's understanding of the effects of the Christ event by exploring a particular image.

3. To recognize the importance of the collection for the Jerusalem churches and what it might reveal about Paul's view of church.

4. To discover what an apostle was in the first century and how early Christians might have determined the authenticity of an apostle.

5. To imaginatively describe their impressions of Paul. This exercise may help the students sort out their own attitudes to Paul. It may reveal more about the individual student than it does about Paul!

Suggested Lecture Topics

– Brief summary of the scholarly problems concerning the unity and structure of this letter.

– Situation in the Corinthian community that occasions this letter.

– Overview of the major themes of the letter: apostleship, God's salvation as reconciliation, collection for the Jerusalem community.

– The role of apostles in the early church communities.

– Paul's concern to defend his apostolic authority.

– Paul as an apostle, an ambassador of Christ.

– The humanity of Paul, a person with intense feelings who learned through his sufferings.

SUGGESTED ANSWERS FOR UNIT II.5

1. a. God calls one to this ministry through the working of the Holy Spirit (2 Cor 3:4–6). It is the mercy of God that allows this gift to be given (2 Cor 4:1).

    b. The frailty of the human minister demonstrates that it is God's power alone that is at work. Divine power shines through human weakness. For Paul, the divine presence was evident in the weakness (suffering/death) of Jesus, and so too, in the frailty of the human minister (2 Cor 4:7–12).

2. a. Some reasons why Paul might recommend that the Corinthian community members be ambassadors of Christ witnessing to reconciliation are:

    *   Their rivalries over leadership by Paul, Apollos, Cephas, or Christ (1 Cor 1:11–13; 3:1–9)

    *   Concern for those who are associating with sexually immoral persons (1 Cor 5:9–13)

    *   Tension over those who are eating food sacrificed to idols (1 Cor 8:1–13)

    *   Divisions regarding their coming together for the Lord's supper (1 Cor 11:17–34)

    *   Tension over whether Paul should visit the community again; Paul wrote to them about the tension (2 Cor 1:23—2:4)

    *   Concern that Paul is not a true apostle (2 Cor 10)

3. a. Three motives that Paul used:

    *   Paul suggests that the community look to the Macedonians who, though poor themselves, had been willing to give beyond the limit of their means. This generosity is a grace from God and should be emulated (2 Cor 8:1–5).

    *   Paul compliments the good character of the Corinthians who are asked to give not because of a command but rather as a test of love (2 Cor 8:7–8).

    *   Paul proposes a motive based on christological considerations (i.e., the attitude of Christ to which 2 Corinthians 8:9 refers). If Christ could give up his rightful riches to become poor that all may be saved (thus actually sharing his riches), so too the Corinthians should share what material riches they have with their fellow Christians. As they are rich, so should they share as Christ did.

    c. If the Jerusalem church accepts the collection, they are accepting Paul's mission. If the Jerusalem church rejects the collection, they are rejecting Paul's mission. Put another way, if the Jerusalem church rejects Paul's mission, they should reject the collection. If the Jerusalem church accepts Paul's mission, they should accept the collection.

4. Using himself as an example, Paul speaks of a true apostle as one who suffers for Christ and as Christ did, and who can boast only of personal weakness, knowing that therein lies strength (2 Cor 11:22—12:10). Also, the true apostle has great love for the community (2 Cor 11:28-29). The false apostle is concerned with the wonders he performs, relying on his own power and awe-inspiring abilities (2 Cor 11:12-15).

II.6
Galatians

Assignment Objectives

To enable students:

1. To explain the background of the Galatian community and its problems and to note the solutions that Paul offers in this letter.

2. To become aware of the meaning and place of the Mosaic Law (Torah) for Paul and the early Christian communities, particularly with respect to Gentile converts.

3. To clarify the different perspectives of Judaism and Christianity regarding the Mosaic Law and the gospel in the process of salvation.

4. To describe Paul's understanding of the role of Christ in salvation history.

5. To articulate Paul's understanding of Christian freedom.

6. To see Paul's perspective on the way in which freedom and authority operate together in a community.

7. To locate Galatia and Arabia on a map.

Read Galatians; Kelly, pages 43–47; EDB articles: "Circumcision," "Galatia," "Galatians, Letter to the," "Faith," and "Judaizing"; "The Letters of Paul: Overview—Galatians," #18 in the SUPPLEMENTARY READINGS at the back of the student workbook

Rationale for Student Questions

To enable students:

1. To recognize the differences between Luke's account of Paul's call/conversion and Paul's own account in his letters.
2. To reflect on Paul's view of humanity's right relationship with God, and how it comes about.
3. To examine Paul's use of the Old Testament (different from what we might expect today).
4. To appreciate the filial relationship humanity has with God because of Christ.
5. To recognize Paul's use of spirit and flesh as dimensions of our spiritual life, and to make a personal application of Galatians.
6. To demonstrate a basic understanding of what Paul is saying in this letter.

Suggested Lecture Topics

– Introduction to the letter to the Galatians: who the Galatians are; the problems that occasion this letter; Paul's response.

– Background and meaning of the Mosaic Law (Torah) for the Jews in Paul's time.

– Christian understanding of the role of Mosaic Law:
   • In Paul's time, noting the problems as Christianity opens to the Gentiles.
   • Later in first century, rethinking the place of the Mosaic Law as Christianity breaks from Judaism (a preview of some of the difficulties in the gospel communities of Matthew and John).
   • In light of the Christian reinterpretation of the Old Testament as Christianity develops into a religion of its own.

– Paul's understanding of justification by faith.

– Paul's use of scripture to make his arguments.

– Paul's view of Christian spiritual life (spirit-flesh polarities).

SUGGESTED ANSWERS FOR UNIT II.6

1. a. Note: there is no horse mentioned in any version of the story. Significant similarities and differences include:

Elements of Story	Acts 9:1–19	Acts 22:1–21	Acts 26:12–18
Type of writing	Narrative	Speech	Speech
Addressees	Luke's audience	To Jewish people	To King Agrippa
Jesus' initial statements	"Saul, Saul, why do you persecute me?" "I am Jesus, whom you are persecuting."	"Saul, Saul, why are you persecuting me?" "I am Jesus of Nazareth, whom you are persecuting."	"Saul, Saul, why are you persecuting me?" "I am Jesus, whom you are persecuting." (Jesus speaks in Hebrew and says more, quoting a Greek proverb.)
Who falls to the ground	Paul falls to the ground.	Paul falls to the ground.	Paul and companions fall to the ground.
What Paul's companions heard and/or saw	Paul's companions heard the voice but saw no one.	Paul's companions saw the light but did not hear anyone.	No mention of companions hearing or seeing anything
What initially happens to Paul	Paul is blinded and is taken to Ananias.	Paul is blinded and is taken to Ananias.	No mention of Ananias
Paul's baptism	Paul is baptized.	Paul is baptized.	No mention of baptism

b. In Galatians 1:11–17 and 1 Corinthians 9:1; 15:8, Paul never mentions Ananias or any other human beings. He is content to demonstrate that he was called by God for this ministry. Both Paul's letters and Acts of the Apostles make it clear that Paul's call was at God's initiative. Jesus appeared to Paul; God was pleased to reveal his son to Paul.

2. Faith in the Christ places humanity in a right relationship with God. Nothing else has the power to effect that right relationship.

3. a. Genesis claims Abraham was justified by faith before he was circumcised. Moreover, the Mosaic Law was given hundreds of years later. Paul uses Abraham as an example of one who is justified by faith, apart from the Law.

   b. The function of the Law in the past was to be a guardian until the age of the Messiah (Gal 3:24–26) by pointing out sin (Gal 3:19).

   c. The Law is no longer applicable because we are in the age of the Messiah (Gal 3:19, 24).

4. Christ's death has rescued humankind from the condition of slavery to Law and allowed us to have the status of children of God and so heirs of the promise. The Father sends the Spirit who dwells in our hearts that we may cry out to God, "Abba."

II.7
Romans 1–4

Assignment Objectives

To enable students:

1. To recognize the social, historical, and religious situation of the Roman community.

2. To appreciate Romans as a profound summary of Paul's Christian message.

3. To become familiar with the structure and themes of Romans.

4. To become aware of Paul's message of justification and why he speaks of it as he does to this Roman community.

5. To define *justification* as God's action through Christ to bring us into a right relationship with God, with our response to this divine action being faith.

6. To explain Paul's view that justification comes from faith in Christ and not from observance of the Mosaic Law.

7. To locate Rome on a map.

Read

Romans 1–4; Kelly, pages 69–72; EDB articles: "Justification," "Righteousness," and "Romans, Letter to the"; "The Letters of Paul: Overview—Romans," #18 in the SUPPLEMENTARY READINGS at the back of the student workbook

Rationale for Student Questions

To enable students:

1. To grasp Paul's view of the Gentile peoples as related to God.
2. To grasp Paul's view of the Jewish people as related to God.
3. To be aware of the broad outlines of Paul's theology by discovering Paul's view of who God is, what God does, how humanity ought to respond to God's initiative.
4. To understand Paul's use of Abraham in his argument regarding justification by faith.
5. To bring Paul's theology to bear on modern issues regarding law and salvation.
6. To engage in personal reflection on the biblical text.

Suggested Lecture Topics

– The Roman Christian community and its situation.

– Romans as highlighting aspects of Paul's gospel message, but not a summary (e.g., no Eucharist, little ecclesiology).

– How Romans develops themes found in Galatians.

– Explanation of Paul's use of the term *justification* in the context of this letter and how it applies to our lives today.

– Justification by faith in Christ apart from works of the Mosaic Law.

SUGGESTED ANSWERS FOR UNIT II.7

1. a. The Gentiles have had the possibility of recognizing God in creation. The invisible things of God (attributes, etc.) are made visible through creation (Rom 1:19–23).

   b. The Gentiles have failed to live according to the moral order implied by their knowledge of God (Rom 1:21–23). Therefore, their thinking has become vain and empty and their minds darkened. The specific sin, idolatry, becomes evident in Romans 1:23. The malice of this choice is clear in its effects on their lives. Also, the Gentiles encourage others to live the same way (Rom 1:32). Therefore, the Gentiles are under the "wrath of God" (Rom 1:18–32) as they are caught up within their own sinful futility, from which only God through Christ can free them.

2. a. The Jewish knowledge of God consists primarily in that they "were entrusted with the oracles of God" (Rom 3:2). God has given them the Law to know his will and what is right (Rom 2:18). Circumcision is a sign of their relationship with God (Rom 2:25–29).

   b. While the Jews boast about the Law, they fail to keep it (Rom 2:23). Circumcision is of no value if one does not fulfill the moral implications of its acceptance (Rom 2:25–29). In summary, the Jews are no better off than the Gentiles in that they, too, are under God's wrath.

3. a. Faced with humanity that has merited God's wrath, God instead responds with righteousness (i.e., God's free gift of establishing humanity in a right relationship with God). God has done this through the Christ and through the gift of faith (Rom 3:21–26).

   b. Humanity's proper response to God's free gift is faith in the Christ. By faith in Christ and not by any other means are human beings brought into a right relationship with God.

4. a. Abraham believed before he was circumcised. It was not his adherence to the Law, but rather his faith in the promise that was "reckoned to him as righteousness" (Rom 4:3b).

> Romans has affected later Christian theology more than any other New Testament book. Scarcely an area of theological development has not been influenced by its teaching. Its influence is manifest even in other NT writings (1 Pet., Heb., Jas.) and subapostolic works (Clement, Ignatius, Polycarp, Justin). Patristic and scholastic commentaries abound. ...Immeasurable is the part Romans played in Reformation debates.... Modern religious thinking has also been greatly affected by the theological commentaries....The contribution that Romans has made to Western Christian thinking is inestimable."
>
> —Joseph A. Fitzmyer, S.J., "Romans,"
> in the New Jerome Biblical Commentary, 51:12

II.8
Romans 5–16

Assignment Objectives

To enable students:

1. To become familiar with Paul's view of Christian life.

2. To describe Paul's view of the role of the Spirit in the life of the Christian.

3. To recognize the way Paul uses scripture to support his ideas.

4. To explain Paul's view of the continuing role of the Jews in God's plan.

5. To recognize the distinction Paul makes between Adam and Christ.

6. To apply the Christian message to practical life situations.

Read   Romans 5–16; Kelly, pages 72–79; EDB articles: "Election: New Testament" and "Deaconess"

Rationale for Student Questions

To enable students:

1. To recognize that Paul makes a comparison between humanity in Adam and humanity in Christ to discuss the superabundant effects of what God has done for humanity in Christ.

2. To appreciate Paul's theological insight regarding baptism.

3. To describe Paul's concept of the Spirit and its relation to the life of the Christian, and to make a connection with their lives.

4. To understand Paul's theological solution and reflections about a practical issue regarding the relationship between Israel and God.

5. To consider the Christian's relation to civil law and to note that this view reflects the time and the situation of the community.

Suggested Lecture Topics

– Original sin and Romans 5:12 vis-à-vis Paul's insistence that what God has done for humanity in Christ is superabundant when compared to the situation in which humanity currently finds itself.

– Spiritual life as Paul sees it. Our Christian response to God's saving initiative.

– The many effects of the Christ event as Paul sees it.

– Paul's understanding of sanctification as God's action through the Holy Spirit for the transformation of humanity and all creation.

– Relationship between Judaism and Christianity then and now.

– Phoebe and the role of women in the early church and today.

– Applying the scripture message to everyday life.

SUGGESTED ANSWERS FOR UNIT II.8

1. a. The human condition under Adam leads to sin and death (Rom 5:12).

   b. The human condition under Christ is grace leading to eternal life (Rom 5:21).

2. For Paul, the Christian is baptized into Christ's death and rises with Christ to new life. Christians are now dead to sin and alive for God in Christ Jesus.

3. a. The Spirit sets us free from the law of sin and death through the Son who came "in the likeness of sinful flesh...to deal with sin" (Rom 8:3b). That same Spirit helps give life to our mortal bodies (Rom 8:10b) and assists us in submitting to God's law (Rom 8:7). The Spirit makes us children of God so that we will not fall into slavery (Rom 8:14-15). We have the first fruits of the Spirit that help us wait in hope for the redemption of our bodies (Rom 8:23-24). Lastly, the Spirit helps us when we are weak and intercedes for us before God (Rom 8:26-27).

4. a. God keeps his promises to Israel (Rom 11:29). Since God's word does not fail (Rom 9:6), Israel has stumbled despite enjoying special privileges of divine favor (Rom 9:4); nevertheless, these privileges have not brought her to faith (Rom 9:1-3).

   b. Paul, using the example of Moses and Pharaoh (Rom 9:14-18), illustrates that God's election is not unjust. God's choices are entirely free as God acts toward the accomplishment of salvation history (Rom 9:17). God is free like the potter (Rom 9:19-24) to choose whomever, whether Jew or Gentile.

   c. The olive tree is a metaphor for the people of God. Paul uses the metaphor to illustrate that the Gentiles have been made part of the people of God. However, just as easily as they were grafted in, they may also be lopped off. Thus, the Gentiles should not be haughty (Rom 11:16-24).

   d. Paul has hope that all Israel will be saved (Rom 11:26). The stumbling of Israel is not definitive (Rom 11:1-36) but permits conversion of the Gentiles (Rom 11:11-15). God's mysterious plan is such that the Gentiles were disobedient to God but then shown mercy. Now some of the Jews are disobedient but they too will be shown mercy. Thus, God allows all to fall into disobedience so that he might show mercy to all (Rom 11:25-32).

5. a. Both Paul and Mark recognize God as the supreme authority (Rom 13:1; Mark 12:17). Both encourage the payment of taxes to the lawful authority (Rom 13:7a; Mark 12:17a). Paul argues that governing authorities are good because they have been appointed by God (Rom 13:2a), while in Mark's gospel, those who ask about the taxes are hypocrites trying to trap Jesus (Mark 12:15). Paul makes it clear that if people do good they are not to fear the governing authority, while Mark does not speak of ruler/subject attitudes toward each other.

Paul's letter to the Romans, as someone has said, "is the profoundest work in existence; it is the cathedral of Christian faith." For theologians, it is the Mount Everest of the New Testament, dared by many, conquered by few. It forces them to stretch their minds, take only the grand perspectives, and look only at cosmic theological maps.... Despite an avalanche of commentaries, studies, monographs, and dissertations, Romans remains the unconquered peak of New Testament studies. Let the reader beware!

—Peter F. Ellis, Seven Pauline Letters

II.9
Colossians; Ephesians; Philemon

Assignment Objectives

To enable students:

1. To explain why Pauline authorship of Colossians and Ephesians is disputed.

2. To recognize the social, historical, and religious situations of the communities to which these letters were sent.

3. To identify the major themes that are found in Paul's letters to the Colossians, the Ephesians, and Philemon.

4. To articulate the unique role of Christ in salvation history as expressed in Colossians and Ephesians.

5. To recognize the rhetorical skill of Paul in his letter to Philemon.

6. To locate Colossae and Ephesus on a map.

Read

Colossians; Ephesians; Philemon; Kelly, pages 47–48 and 203–11; EDB article: "Marriage"; "The Letters of Paul: Overview—Colossians, Ephesians, Philemon," #18, "Ten Effects of the Christ Event," #22, and "Self-Quiz on Paul—2," #23, in the SUPPLEMENTARY READINGS at the back of the student workbook

Rationale for Student Questions

To enable students:
1. To appreciate the Christology of Colossians.
2. To recognize early marks of Christian unity and analyze their suitability for today.
3. To deal with a problematic passage by trying to distinguish what the text meant to the original audience in their context and what the passage may mean to audiences now.
4. To appreciate the historical and continued relevance of Paul's message for today.
5. To make a personal appropriation of the material studied.

Suggested Lecture Topics

– Problems of the Pauline authorship of Colossians and Ephesians.

– Background to Colossians, Ephesians, and Philemon (e.g., where communities were located, situations that occasioned the letters).

– Images of church presented in Colossians and Ephesians:
   • Movement from the particular communities to the universal church
   • Differences between these images of church and other New Testament images already seen

– Dealing with problematic texts, recalling that the meaning of scripture depends on the context in which we understand it, for example:
   • Differences between marriage in the first century (often contractual by families, no love necessary) and marriage today (often commitment by individuals, love is presupposed)
   • United States Conference of Catholic Bishops, "When I Call for Help: A Pastoral Response to Domestic Violence Against Women"—A Statement of the U.S. Catholic Bishops (United States Catholic Conference, Inc., 2002)
   • Differences between slavery in the first century (not racially based) and slavery in modern times.

SUGGESTED ANSWERS FOR UNIT II.9

1. a. Christ is:

   - The image of the unseen God (Col 1:15)

   - One who is supreme over all creation (Col 1:15)

   - One who existed before anything else (Col 1:17)

   - Head of the church, which is his body (Col 1:18)

   - Firstborn from the dead (Col 1:18)

   - One in whom all perfection is found (Col 1:19)

   b. Christ is the principle of unity in the universe (Col 1:17) and agent of creation; everything was created in him, through him, and for him (Col 1:16). By his death on the cross all is reconciled through him and for him (Col 1:20).

2. a. One body, one spirit, one hope, one Lord, one faith, one baptism, one God and Father of all.

If we suppose that Paul, as is very likely, used the hieratic papyrus, he could get about 140 words on each sheet. Various references in ancient authors indicate that it took about one minute to write three syllables and an hour for seventy two words. Naturally these figures are approximate, but taking them as the average and as a basis, we find that the earliest epistle, 1 Thessalonians which was 1472 words, must have taken ten sheets of papyrus and more than twenty hours' writing time. The longest epistle, that to the Romans, which contains 7101 words, required fifty sheets and more than ninety-eight hours' writing time. The shortest, Philemon, required almost three sheets and four hours.

—Giuseppe Ricciotti, Paul the Apostle

II.10
Unit Two Review

Students will be responsible for:

1. A memory verse from Acts of the Apostles or one of the Pauline letters studied in this unit, indicating the translation used and citing reference.

2. The information included in the following SUPPLEMENTARY READINGS at the back of the student workbook:
   - #8. "Luke-Acts: Overview"
   - #18. "The Letters of Paul: Overview"
   - #21. "Self-Quiz on Acts of the Apostles and Paul—1"
   - #22. "Ten Effects of the Christ Event"
   - #23. "Self-Quiz on Paul—2"

3. The location of the following places and areas on the map "The World of Paul," #16 in the SUPPLEMENTARY READINGS at the back of the student workbook:

Antioch in Syria	Corinth	Ephesus	Rome
Athens	Crete	Galatia	Tarsus
Colossae	Cyprus	Macedonia	Thessalonica
	Damascus	Philippi	

Suggested Lecture Topics

- Review the basic information on Acts of the Apostles, emphasizing its connection to Luke's gospel: authorship, structure, themes, and concerns.
- Review Paul—the man, his historical situation, the general themes of the letters.
- Recall that Paul's experience is a key to what was happening to the church from Jesus' death (ca. AD 30) to the time of the gospels (ca. AD 70).
- Review the geography of the Hellenistic Mediterranean world.
- Using one or two main themes, point out the relevance of Paul's message for students today.

Name _____

Center _____ Group # _____

1. Acts of the Apostles was written by _____ about the year(s) _____ for a

community composed primarily of _____ in order to _____

_____

_____.

.

2. Paul was born in the city of _____. Educated at the feet of Gamaliel, Paul became a

member of the _____ party. He encountered the risen Lord on the road to

_____. According to Christian tradition, Paul was martyred outside the city of

_____ about the year _____.

3. Identify the letters in which these themes are a PRIMARY CONCERN for Paul:

_____   Freedom in Christ and the *different gospel* of salvation preached by Judaizers

_____   Divisions within the community; church as the Body of Christ having many
members; charismatic gifts; resurrection of the dead

_____   Watchfulness in view of the imminent return of Christ; concern over whether
those already dead are better or worse off than those alive at the time of Christ's
return

_____   Justification by faith in Christ apart from works of the Mosaic Law; concern
about why many Jews have not become Christians

_____   Christ's place in the universe as supreme over all; false teachers encourage as-
ceticism and the worship of angels

_____   Christians are to "have the mind of Christ" in his attitude of *kenosis* (i.e., "self-
emptying")

_____   About a slave who is now a Christian and so a "brother in the Lord"

_____ Paul defends his apostleship; God's act of salvation as an act of reconciliation; concern for the collection for the Jerusalem church

_____ Has Christ already come? Signs that must precede Christ's second coming

_____ God's plan for salvation; the universal church with Christ as its head; Gentiles are included now to form a building with Christ as the cornerstone

4. Give a brief description of justification by faith in Christ as it is used by Paul.

5. Briefly explain two of the following images that Paul uses to discuss the effects of the Christ event for humanity: Expiation, Sanctification, Redemption, Freedom, Reconciliation, Salvation, New Creation, Transformation, Glorification.

6. Explain what you consider to be Paul's most important contribution to today's church. Make sure you offer some reasons for your choice.

7. Write your memory verse from Acts of the Apostles or one of the Pauline letters. Include reference and translation used.

8. What is the most significant thing you have learned during your study of Acts of the Apostles and the Pauline letters?

MAP

In the map on the facing page, please fill in the following locations:

Philippi	Crete
Colossae	Antioch in Syria
Rome	Thessalonica
Galatia	Tarsus
Damascus	Ephesus
Corinth	

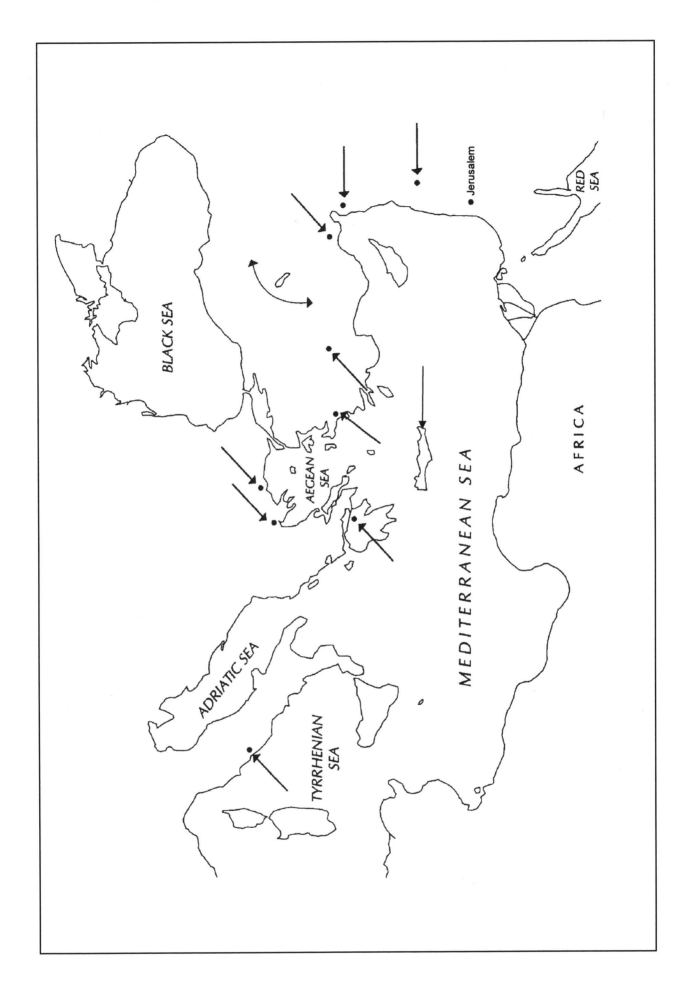

BLACK SEA

RED SEA

Jerusalem

AEGEAN SEA

MEDITERRANEAN SEA

AFRICA

ADRIATIC SEA

TYRRHENIAN SEA

63

ANSWERS TO YEAR TWO–UNIT TWO TEST

1. Luke; AD 80–90; Gentile Christians; continue major themes begun in Luke's gospel; present his understanding of salvation history by showing how the ministry and mission of the church continues the ministry and mission of Jesus in Luke's gospel

2. Tarsus, Pharisee, Damascus, Rome, AD 65–68

3. Galatians
   1 Corinthians
   1 Thessalonians
   Romans
   Colossians
   Philippians
   Philemon
   2 Corinthians
   2 Thessalonians
   Ephesians

4. Justification is an image taken from the legal sphere (acquittal of a guilty person) to describe God's action through Christ to reestablish the right relationship between God and all humanity.

5. See "Ten Effects of the Christ Event," #22 in the SUPPLEMENTARY READINGS.

6. Many possibilities.

7. Any passage from Acts of the Apostles or one of the Pauline letters. Reference and translation used must be included.

8. Many possibilities.

MAP
(reading from left to right)

    Rome

    Corinth (south of Thessalonica)

    Thessalonica

    Philippi

    Crete

    Ephesus

    Colossae

    Galatia

    Tarsus

    Antioch in Syria

    Damascus

UNIT III
Jesus: Johannine Views

Objectives

To enable students:

1. To recall the chronology, geography, and social and cultural environment of early Christianity as reflected in the Johannine writings.

2. To recognize the Christian message through an investigation of the structure, themes, and theology of John's gospel, the Johannine letters, and the Book of Revelation.

3. To analyze the Gospel of John using the historical-critical method, including literary criticism, form criticism, and redaction criticism.

4. To apply the methods of biblical criticism to the writings of apocalyptic Christianity in order to interpret their meaning.

Textbooks

Primary Text: The Bible. Use a good translation with scholarly notes.

Other Texts: For helpful background and handy reference we recommend:
Eerdmans *Dictionary of the Bible* (cited as EDB)
Hammond's *Atlas of the Bible Lands* (cited as Hammond Atlas)
Joseph F. Kelly, *An Introduction to the New Testament for Catholics* (cited as Kelly)
Raymond E. Brown, SS, *The Gospel and Letters of John: A Concise Commentary* (cited as Brown)
Kurt Aland, ed., *Synopsis of the Four Gospels*
Craig R. Koester, *Revelation and the End of All Things* (cited as Koester)

Assignments

Each lesson is to be studied by the students in preparation for their group discussion. For each biblical passage, students study the biblical text and footnotes for that particular passage, do other assigned readings, and answer the written work *on a separate page*.

III.1   JOHN 1–4

III.2   JOHN 5–12

III.3   JOHN 13–17

III.4   JOHN 18–21

III.5   1 JOHN; 2 JOHN; 3 JOHN

III.6   APOCALYPTIC CHRISTIANITY: MARK 13; LUKE 21; MATTHEW 24–25

III.7   REVELATION 1–3

III.8   REVELATION 4–14

III.9   REVELATION 15–22

III.10 UNIT THREE REVIEW

UNIT THREE TEST

III.1
John 1–4

Assignment Objectives

To enable students:

1. To explain why John's gospel was written.

2. To become familiar with the social, historical, and religious situation of the Johannine community.

3. To describe the tension between Christianity and Judaism after the destruction of the temple and see John's gospel as a response to this tension.

4. To recognize the distinctive structure, themes, and message of John's gospel and to note how it is different from the synoptic gospels.

5. To better understand the person of Jesus and the faith of those who come to Jesus.

Read   John 1–4; Kelly, pages 157–64; Brown, pages 9–39; EDB articles: "John, Gospel of"; "The Gospel According to John and the Johannine Letters: Overview—The Gospel According to John," #24, and "Johannine Vocabulary," #25, in the SUPPLEMENTARY READINGS at the back of the student workbook

Rationale for Student Questions

To enable students:
1. To appreciate John's use of high Christology as summarized in the Prologue.
2. To distinguish between the call narratives of John and Mark.
3. To reflect on the identity of Jesus by utilizing a specific story recorded in John's gospel.
4. To study the faith-response of one of characters in John 1–4.
5. To apply John 1–4 to their personal experience.

Suggested Lecture Topics

- Situation of the Johannine community, especially its relationship to Judaism and to the communities represented by the synoptic gospels.
- Specific differences between John's gospel and the synoptic gospels.
- Christology of John's gospel in relationship to that of the synoptic gospels and Paul, noting especially the issue of the preexistence of the Word and the Word's incarnation.
- Author's use of symbolism and polarities (e.g., light versus darkness).
- John's Prologue as a prelude to and summary of themes in John's gospel.
- Ability of the author to dramatize personal encounters with Jesus.

SUGGESTED ANSWERS FOR UNIT III.1

1. From the Prologue of John (John 1:1–18) we learn that:

   a. The Word:

   - Was (in the beginning [John 1:1])

   - Was with God in a special relationship from all eternity (John 1:1–2)

   - Was God (John 1:1). The climax of John 1:1 proclaims that the Word, although being distinct from God, is on a level of equality with God, participating in divinity.

   - Is source and agent of creation, life in general, and eternal life (John 1:3–4, 10)

   - Is the light (John 1:4–5, 8–9)

   - Is the only Son of God who is close to the Father's heart (John 1:18)

   b. The Word:

   - (As the light) shines in the darkness, illuminates humankind with the true revelation of God (John 1:5, 9)

   - Came into the world and gives to those who receive the Word and believe in his name the power to become children of God (John 1:10–12)

   - Became flesh and pitched a tent (dwelled) among his people (John 1:14)

   - Shares the fullness of grace and truth with all humankind (John 1:16)

   - Makes the Father known (John 1:18)

2.

John 1:35–51	Mark 1:16–20
John the Baptist points Jesus out and two of John's disciples, Andrew and one unnamed, follow Jesus (1:35, 40)	Simon and Andrew, the first called, are not disciples of John the Baptist (1:16)
Andrew and the unnamed disciple follow Jesus when John says Jesus is the Lamb of God (1:36b)	No indication of why the disciples follow Jesus
They question Jesus about where he lives and are invited to "come and see" (1:38–39)	No question about where Jesus lives
It is implied that they follow immediately (1:37)	The two disciples follow immediately (1:18)
No profession given for either disciple	Simon and Andrew were fishermen (1:16)
Andrew follows Jesus first, then tells his brother Simon he has found the Messiah, and brings Simon to Jesus (1:40–42a)	Both Simon and Andrew are called together to follow Jesus (1:17)
Simon is given a new name—Cephas/Peter (1:42b)	Simon is not renamed
Simon and Andrew are the only disciples called that day; the next day Jesus calls Philip and then Philip gets Nathanael to come and see (1:43–46)	James and John are called on the same day as Simon and Andrew (1:20)

3. a. From the story of the wedding feast at Cana (John 2:1–12), we learn the following about Jesus' identity:

  - Jesus replaces the Jewish purification rites (John 2:6).

  - Jesus is able to change water into wine (John 2:7, 10).

  - Jesus is able to call forth belief (John 2:11c).

  - Jesus is able to reveal his glory (John 2:11b).

  - Jesus is Messiah, the bringer of salvation (note the Messianic images: banquet setting, celebration, and choice wine in abundance [John 2:1–2, 9–10]).

  b. From the story of the cleansing of the temple (John 2:13–22), we learn the following about Jesus' identity:

  - Jesus is son of the Father (John 2:16c).

  - Jesus is consumed by the temple being the house of God (John 2:17).

  - Jesus indicates that the temple of his body will replace the old temple (John 2:21). He will become the focus and "place" of worship (i.e., God meets God's people in the person of Jesus).

If John has been described as the pearl of great price among the New Testament writings, then one may say that the Prologue is the pearl within this gospel.
—Raymond E. Brown, SS

III.2
John 5–12

Assignment objectives

To enable students:

1. To recognize the relationship of Jesus to the Jewish feasts as portrayed in John's gospel.

2. To discover how John understands the divinity and humanity of Jesus.

3. To discover the relationship between the call stories of the various gospels.

4. To reflect upon the use of John's gospel in the Sunday Lectionary.

5. To locate the Pool of Bethesda, Solomon's Portico, the Pool of Siloam, and the Mount of Olives on a map.

Read

John 5–12; Kelly, pages 164–71; Brown, pages 39–70; EDB article: "Sabbath"; "Jewish Calendar and Special Feast Days," #27 in the SUPPLEMENTARY READINGS at the back of the student workbook

Rationale for Student Questions

To enable students:

1. To recognize the similarities and differences between God (Father) and Jesus (Son) as used by this author.

2. To review the Jewish feasts and see how Jesus is fulfilling these feasts and what they symbolize.

3. To recognize the connection of the "I AM" statements with the Jewish sacred name of God.

4. To connect the Bread of Life theme to our current understanding of Eucharist.

5. To appreciate how John's gospel is used in the Lectionary during the Lenten season.

6. To recognize the relationship between the Gospel of John and the synoptic gospels.

Suggested Lecture Topics

– Similarities and differences between the feasts of Judaism and those of Christianity.

– Jewish and Christian conflicts about Jesus as disclosed in John's gospel.

– Utilization of John's gospel in the Lectionary.

SUGGESTED ANSWERS FOR UNIT III.2

1. a. Examples of the evangelist showing that Jesus is equal to God:

   - Jesus has the power to heal "at once" (John 5:8–9).

   - Jesus has the authority to give commands concerning the Sabbath (John 5:10–11).

   - Jesus claims the divine prerogative to work on the Sabbath (John 5:17–18).

   - The Son does everything the Father does (John 5:19b).

   - Jesus is able to do what the Father does, and so honor should be given to the Son (John 5:21).

   - Jesus and the Father are both to be honored (John 5:23).

   - Both the Father and the Son have power to execute judgment (John 5:26–27).

   b. Examples of the evangelist showing that Jesus is subordinate to God:

   - Jesus does not usurp God's power by working independently of God, but acts with complete dependence on the Father (John 5:19a, 30).

   - Jesus always seeks to do the will of the Father (John 5:30b).

   - Jesus was sent to do the will of the Father (John 5:36b).

   - Jesus comes in the Father's name and seeks the glory of the Father (John 5:43–44).

3. For the Jews, the "I AM" statements mean that Jesus is identifying himself with the name of the LORD (Exodus 3:14). This claim to divinity provokes a reaction (John 8:59) equivalent to punishment for blasphemy (see Leviticus 24:16).

6. a.

John 6:1–15	Luke 9:10b–17
Jesus was at the Sea of Tiberias/Galilee (6:1)	Jesus was in Bethsaida (1:10b)
A large crowd followed Jesus because of signs (6:2)	No reason given for following Jesus
On a mountain; the feast of Passover was at hand (6:3–4)	No specific setting in this gospel
No indication given about the teaching of Jesus	Jesus spoke about the kingdom of God (9:11a)
Jesus asks Philip about food to test him (6:5b–6)	Disciples suggest people go away for food (9:12)
Jesus knew what he was going to do (6:6b)	No mention of Jesus' knowledge
Cost of feeding is over 200 denarii (9:7)	No cost given, but concern about buying food (9:13c)

Continued on next page

71

John 6:1–15	Luke 9:10b–17
Andrew finds a boy with five loaves and two fish (6:8–9a)	The twelve indicate that they have no more than five loaves and two fish (9:13b)
5,000 men gathered (6:10b)	5,000 men (9:14a) ordered to sit in groups of 50
Jesus took the loaves/gave thanks/ distributed loaves and fish (6:11)	Jesus took the loaves and fish/looked up to heaven/blessed/broke/gave them to disciples to set before the crowd (9:16a)
All ate their fill (6:12a)	All ate and were satisfied (9:17a)
Gathering fragments so that nothing may be lost (6:12b)	No mention of why fragments gathered
Filled 12 baskets (6:13a)	Filled 12 baskets (9:17b)
People saw this as a sign that Jesus was a prophet and wanted to make him king; but Jesus withdrew by himself (6:14–15)	No mention of these details

b. Theological perspective of John's gospel:

- Jesus knows what he will do; he is in control.

- Connection of the multiplication of the loaves with Passover: Jesus is the true bread of life come down from heaven.

- Nothing/no-one is "lost" from the reign of God.

Theological perspective of Luke's gospel:

- No indication that Jesus knows in advance what he will do.

- The importance of Jesus ushering in the kingdom of God.

- The description of the multiplication of the loaves and fish (i.e., Jesus took, blessed, broke, and gave) is similar to the institution account in Luke 22:19.

III.3
John 13–17

Assignment Objectives

To enable students:

1. To distinguish the Last Supper scene in John from the Last Supper scene in the synoptic gospels, noting that John includes Jesus' farewell discourse and the footwashing scene.

2. To see Jesus' farewell discourse in John's gospel as a guideline for Christian community living.

3. To explain the Johannine understanding of the identity and mission of the Advocate (Paraclete).

4. To describe the Johannine ideal of a Christian community and its mission in the world.

5. To explain the fourth evangelist's understanding of the relationship of his community to different religious groups outside the Johannine community.

Read John 13–17; Kelly, pages 171–73; Brown, pages 71–87; EDB articles: "Footwashing," "Holy Spirit: John," "Paraclete," and "Truth"

Rationale for Student Questions

To enable students:

1. To discover the distinctive Johannine perspective on service and its connection to Eucharist.

2. To recognize the author's perception of Jesus in relationship to the Christian community.

3. To identify the Johannine theology of the Holy Spirit as Advocate/Paraclete, assisting the community to carry out the mission of Jesus.

4. To relate the farewell discourse of John's gospel to a farewell discourse already studied and to apply the form of a farewell discourse in a creative manner.

5. To apply the scriptures to their own experience.

Suggested Lecture Topics

- Connection between the footwashing scene in John 13 and our understanding of Eucharist.

- Literary form of a farewell discourse given before someone's death. Recall the discourses of Jacob (Gen 47:29–49:33), Moses (Book of Deuteronomy), Joshua (Josh 22–24), David (1 Chron 28–29), and Paul (Acts 20:17–38).

- Major themes of Jesus' farewell discourse.

- Person and work of the Holy Spirit in Luke-Acts in comparison to that proclaimed in John's gospel.

- Mission of the Christian community as given in Jesus' farewell discourse in John.

- Application of the farewell discourse in the Gospel of John to personal experience.

SUGGESTED ANSWERS FOR UNIT III.3

1. At the time of his *hour*, Jesus demonstrates his self-giving love and service by washing his disciples' feet. The disciples are called to participate in this act of service in order to be united with Jesus and each other. In Eucharist we accept and make our own what Jesus offers, which enables us to serve as we are served by Jesus Christ himself. Eucharist reveals Jesus the servant who gives up his life out of love for his own and our willingness to be one with Jesus and share in his service of love.

2. The Christian community's relationship with Jesus in John 15:

   • The vine and branches imagery (John 15:1–8) indicates communion of the disciples with Jesus.

   • Disciples cannot bear fruit by themselves (John 15:4) but, if they do bear fruit, they will give glory to the Father of Jesus (John 15:8).

   • If the Christian community keeps Jesus' commandments, it shares in the love that exists between the Father and the Son (John 15:9). This love is so profound that Jesus calls the disciples his friends instead of servants (John 15:14–15).

   The Christian community's relationship with Jesus in John 17:

   • Disciples belong to the Father and to Jesus and Jesus is glorified in them (John 17:9–10).

   • Jesus protected the disciples (John 17:12a) and he will give that same protection to future disciples who also commit themselves to the Father by believing through the disciples' word (John 17:20–21).

   • Perhaps the most important request of Jesus' prayer is for communion among believers—among themselves and with the Father and the Son (John 17:21).

   b. The mission of the Christian community in John 15:

   • Disciples must bear fruit by their work (John 15:5b, 8, 16b).

   • The best way for disciples to bear fruit is to love one another as Jesus loved them (John 15:10, 12, 14, 17).

   • Disciples are to testify to Jesus just as the Advocate does (John 15:27).

   • Belonging to Jesus might cause others to hate the disciples just as Jesus was hated (John 15:18–19).

   The mission of the Christian community in John 17:

   • The mission of the disciples is in the world, where they are to bear witness to Jesus (John 17:15–18).

   • The disciples' goal is to "become completely one" in order to show the world that they were sent by Jesus (John 17:22–23).

3. The Advocate/Paraclete is:

   • The gift from the Father at Jesus' request.

   • Another Advocate who continues Jesus' work.

- The source of truth who abides in the disciples.

- One who consoles the disciples when Jesus departs so they will not be orphaned.

- One who continues to teach the disciples to remind them of everything that Jesus said.

- The presence of the risen Lord in the Lord's absence.

- One who testifies on behalf of Jesus and gives the disciples power to do the same.

- One who convicts the world of its mistake in rejecting Jesus and brings that world to judgment.

- One who guides the disciples into all truth because he will declare the same truth that Jesus did.

III.4
John 18–21

Assignment objectives

To enable students:

1. To recognize how John's passion narrative reinforces the themes and theology of his gospel.

2. To recognize how John's Holy Week chronology differs from that of the synoptic gospels.

3. To describe John's resurrection theology of Jesus and its relationship to the Advocate/Holy Spirit.

4. To describe the prominent theories regarding the identity of the Beloved Disciple (i.e., whether or not he is a real person, a symbolic figure, or a real individual idealized).

5. To comprehend the significance of the Beloved Disciple passages for John's understanding of Christian discipleship.

Read

John 18–21; Kelly, pages 173–78; Brown, pages 87–104; EDB articles: "Beloved Disciple," "Kidron," "Thomas," "Mary: 2. Mary Magdalene"

Rationale for Student Questions

To enable students:

1. To discover the emphasis in John's gospel on Jesus as one in control throughout the passion.
2. To be familiar with a particular detail of John's gospel in relation to the Passover feast.
3. To contrast Jesus' words from the cross in John's gospel with Jesus' words in Mark's gospel, in order to understand better each evangelist's theology.
4. To apply the resurrection narrative of John's gospel to their own life experience.
5. To express in an original, creative manner the impact of John's gospel on them.
6. To recall the purpose of redaction criticism as it applies to John's gospel.

Suggested Lecture Topics

– Major themes and theology of the passion narrative in John's gospel.

– Contrasts between the passion narrative of John and that of Mark and Luke.

– Faith responses to the Risen Lord as illustrated dramatically by the characters in the passion and resurrection accounts of John's gospel.

– Role of the unnamed Beloved Disciple in the Gospel of John.

– The Beloved Disciple in relationship to the Johannine community.

– The Beloved Disciple in relationship to Peter, as Peter is a representative of the church as a whole.

– Redaction of John's gospel by a later author.

SUGGESTED ANSWERS FOR UNIT III.4

1. What is learned about the identity of Jesus from the description of his arrest in the garden includes:

    - Jesus crossing the Kidron Valley (John 18:1) is an allusion to Jesus' kingship. Recall that David crosses the same valley when he flees from Absalom (2 Sam 15:23). Also, the blood of slaughtered Passover lambs washed down into this valley; perhaps an allusion to Jesus as the new lamb of the new Passover.

    - Jesus entered a garden (John 18:1) as the new Adam to confront Satan and evil.

    - Those coming to arrest Jesus carried lanterns and torches (John 18:3). They came in darkness and must use artificial light in order to arrest the one who is the true light.

    - Jesus knew what was going to happen to him (John 18:4) and took the initiative to meet his opponents.

    - Jesus was from Nazareth (John 18:5).

    - Jesus is again identified with the "I AM" of Exodus 3:14 when he says "I am he" (John 18:5b).

    - Jesus was so much in control that they recoiled in fear (John 18:6); nothing can happen to Jesus unless he permits it.

    - Jesus is willing to give himself up for others, but his own must not be lost (John 18:8–9).

    - Jesus accepts the "cup" the Father has given him, thus being an obedient Son (John 18:11). His disciples are powerless in their attempt to interfere with Jesus' hour.

2. Noon was the time that the priests began to slaughter the Passover lambs in the temple; thus, Jesus is the new Passover Lamb.

3. a. In John's gospel, Jesus says:

    - "Woman, here is your son"

    - "Here is your mother."

    - "I am thirsty."

    - "It is finished."

    b. In Mark's gospel, Jesus says only one thing:

    "Eloi, Eloi, lema sabachthani?" ("My God, my God, why have you forsaken me?"). The text also says that he cries out before he dies, but there are no words.

    c. The words of Jesus on the cross in Mark convey that Jesus felt abandoned by God. Also, since Jesus' words are taken from the first line of Psalm 22, they connect the crucifixion to God's ultimate vindication. On the other hand, the writer of John's gospel wants the community—and us—to understand that Jesus is totally in charge of what happens to him and that he is able to build the community of faith from the ground up with his mother and the Beloved Disciple. In that sense, the Beloved Disciple represents each member of the community who recognizes in faith the identity of Jesus and what he came to accomplish. His earthly life can end ("It is finished") with the assurance that the Advocate will be the teacher of truth for the community as it remains faithful to Jesus and all he meant to them.

6. a. John 20:30–31 is an apparent conclusion to the gospel. Yet, another chapter is added. Note that in chapter 21:

- The sons of Zebedee are mentioned for the first time in the gospel (John 21:2).

- Jesus is not recognized even though the disciples saw him twice in chapter 20 (John 21:4).

- There is the story of the rehabilitation of Peter.

- There is an explanation of the death of the Beloved Disciple before the return of Jesus (John 21:20–23).

- There is an ending (John 21:25) that is similar to John 20:30.

John's Passion story asserts what is a basic conviction of the entire New Testament: the death and resurrection of Jesus have robbed death of its sting.... Evocative images of homecoming, of reunion, and final rest ransack the terror of death.... Without knowing its immediate source, generation after generation of Christians has faced death with peace on the basis of these Gospel images and the faith they express.

—Donald Senior, CP

III.5
1 John; 2 John; 3 John

Assignment Objectives

To enable students:

1. To become familiar with the historical, social, literary, and theological situation that generated the letters of John.

2. To appreciate the issues related to the authorship of the letters of John.

3. To recognize how the letters of John reflect the issues and points of controversy that led to the fragmentation of the Johannine community.

4. To identify the contributions of the Johannine letters to the social and theological development of early Christianity.

Read

1 John; 2 John; 3 John; Kelly, pages 239–46; Brown, pages 105–26; EDB articles: "John, Letters of," and "Antichrist"; "The Gospel According to John and the Johannine Letters: Overview—The Johannine Letters," #24, and "The History of the Johannine Community," #28, in the SUPPLEMENTARY READINGS at the back of the student workbook

Rationale for Student Questions

To enable students:

1. To investigate the style of a prologue and apply it to their own experience.
2. To recognize John's way of addressing sin in the lives of believers.
3. To identify the role of the antichrist in 1 John and compare it to modern concepts with which students might be familiar.
4. To investigate a major theme of 1 John.
5. To identify a significant theme of 2 John.
6. To apply the advice of the Johannine letters to their own personal experience.

Suggested Lecture Topics

– The three Johannine letters in the context of the Johannine community: history, social situation, and theological emphases of that community.

– Scholarly opinions about authorship of the letters of John.

– Basic structure of the Johannine letters.

– How the Johannine letters address the concerns of the Johannine Christian community in the first century.

– Important theological themes of the letters of John.

– Themes of the Johannine letters compared to themes of John's gospel.

– Some issues of these letters and their relationship to other writings in the scriptures.

SUGGESTED ANSWERS FOR UNIT III.5

1. a. Important issues for the author of 1 John include the following:

    • The author of 1 John includes himself among those who preserve and develop the authentic testimony of the Beloved Disciple, the source of John's gospel (1 John 1:1).

    • The testimony proclaimed concerns the word of *life* (i.e., the proclamation of divine life made visible in and through Jesus [1 John 1:1–2]).

    • The purpose of the proclamation is that the readers of 1 John participate in divine life and have fellowship with the Father and his Son, Jesus Christ (and have fellowship with those who proclaim the divine life [1 John 1:3–4]).

2. Regarding the problem of sin in the lives of the believers:

    • Sin is cleansed by the blood of Jesus, Son of the Father, who is faithful and just and forgives us (1 John 1:7, 9).

    • We deceive ourselves, do not have truth within us, and make God a liar if we declare that we have not sinned (1 John 1:8, 10).

    • We are to acknowledge our sins to be forgiven (1 John 1:9).

    • Jesus, our advocate with the Father, atones for our sins and those of the whole world with his sacrifice (1 John 2:1b, 2).

3. a. The antichrist to come in the future seems to be one person, but there were many "antichrists...who have come." They did not stay with the community.

    b. The major characteristic is that the antichrist denies both "the Father and the Son" (1 John 2:22b).

4. a. God's love (1 John 4:9, 19); our love for one another (1 John 4:7, 11, 12, 20) our love for God (1 John 4:20).

    b. God's love is basic. 1 John emphasizes that God loved us first (1 John 4:10, 19).

    c. God's love is revealed by sending his only Son to the world that we might have life through him (1 John 4:9) and as an "atoning sacrifice for our sins" (1 John 4:10). Also, the one sent by God gave us his Spirit (1 John 4:13).

5. They are deceivers because they "do not confess that Jesus Christ has come in the flesh" (2 John 7a) and do not "abide in the teaching of Christ, but [go] beyond it" (2 John 9a).

III.6
Apocalyptic Christianity:
Mark 13; Luke 21; Matthew 24–25

Assignment Objectives:

To enable students:

1. To describe apocalyptic literature, its purpose, its characteristics, its relation to Judaism and the Old Testament, and the types of situations that give rise to it.
2. To understand why some Christians in the first-century communities connected the destruction of the Jerusalem temple by the Romans in AD 70 with the end of the world.
3. To recognize that apocalyptic material does not foretell how the world will end, but imagines how God might triumph over evil.
4. To distinguish between eschatology and apocalypticism.
5. To analyze the apocalyptic passages found in the synoptic gospels.

Read

Mark 13; Luke 21; Matthew 24–25; Kelly, pages 102–3 and 128–29; EDB articles: "Apocalyptic," "Parousia," and "Eschatology: Jesus and the Gospels"; "Apocalyptic Literature as Dramatic Imagination," #30 in the SUPPLEMENTARY READINGS at the back of the student workbook

Rationale for Student Questions

To enable students:

1. To analyze the apocalyptic material in each of the synoptic gospels and notice its relationship to the destruction of the Jerusalem temple (AD 70).
2. To find a message of hope, the primary virtue stressed in apocalyptic literature, in the apocalyptic chapters of the synoptic gospels.
3. To discover the basic message in the apocalyptic passage of each synoptic gospel and to apply that message to their own life experience.
4. To utilize imagination by writing a short apocalyptic passage.
5. To use their own life experience to appreciate the anxiety of first-century Jews and Christians with regard to the significance of the temple's end.

Suggested Lecture Topics

– Apocalyptic worldview as an imaginative way of providing hope that God will triumph over evil.
– Apocalyptic literature as one type of eschatological writing.
– Apocalyptic literature as a faith response to a situation of crisis for the community of faith.
– Basic characteristics of apocalyptic literature:
  • Usually pseudonymous
  • Always some element of vision
  • Appearance of a heavenly mediator to facilitate understanding of the vision
  • Use of disguised, cryptic, or symbolic language (e.g., names, numbers, beasts, colors)
  • Repetition of the same message through the presentation of grand symbolic scenes
– Literary apocalyptic works in Judaism and Christianity.
– Daniel 7:9–14 as background to the eschatological image of "one like a human being" (Son of Man).

SUGGESTED ANSWERS FOR UNIT III.6

1. a.

	Mark 13	Luke 21	Matthew 24–25
a. To whom is Jesus speaking?	Privately to Peter, James, John, and Andrew (13:3)	Them?—could be disciples (see 20:45)	Disciples (24:3)
b. Where does Jesus speak?	Mount of Olives opposite the temple (13:3)	At the temple (21:5–7)	Mount of Olives (24:3)
c. Questions asked of Jesus	Two questions are asked: "Tell us, when will this be…?" "…what will be the sign that all these things are about to be accomplished?" (13:4)	Two questions are asked: "Teacher, when will this be…?" "…what will be the sign that this is about to take place?" (21:7)	Two questions are asked: "Tell us, when will this be…?" "…what will be the sign of your coming and of the end of the age?" (24:3)
d. Signs preceding temple destruction	The signs are in Mark 13:5–20; unique to Mark is that the gospel must *first* be preached (13:10).	These signs are in Luke 21:8–24; unique to Luke is the fall of Jerusalem (21:20, 24); they will lay their hands on you (21:15a); you will be given wisdom (21:15); they will fall on the sword and will be led captive (21:24a); not a hair of your head will perish (21:18).	The signs are in Matthew 24:4–22; unique to Matthew is false prophets arising (24:11); many of these signs are in Matthew 10:17–22a; the desolating sacrilege is spoken of by Daniel (24:15); parable of the ten virgins (25:1–13); the last judgment scene (25:31–46)
e. When will the Son of Man come?	When you see these things happening (13:29); no one knows the day nor the hour; before this generation passes away (13:30, 32–33, 35)	When you see these things taking place the kingdom of God is near (21:31); before this generation passes away (21:32)	When you see all these things, the Son of Man is near (24:33); no one knows day nor the hour (24:36, 42); this generation will not pass away (24:34, 25:13)
f. Signs preceding the coming of the Son of Man	The signs are in Mark 13:21–25	The signs are in Luke 21:24–25	The signs are in Matthew 24:23–31
g. How to use time until end?	Preach the gospel (13:10); do not worry, the Holy Spirit will speak through the faithful (13:11); be alert (13:23, 33–34); keep awake (13:35–37)	Take heed, don't be weighed down with things of this life, watch at all times, pray (21:34–36)	Keep awake and be ready (24:42, 44); be vigilant, use time and gifts of God properly and responsibly (24:45—25:30); concretely and actively love, give and show mercy (25:31–46)

2. Specific ways in which the evangelists provide hope for their communities by including these passages in their gospels:

Mark 13:

The one who endures persecution and trials to the end will be saved (Mark 13:13). Those who remain faithful will be counted among the elect at the end time (Mark 13:27).

Luke 21:

Luke includes much of Mark.

Luke adds: "Now when these things begin to take place, stand up and raise your heads, because your redemption is drawing near" (Luke 21:28). Also note Luke 21:31, 33, 36.

Matthew 24–25:

Matthew repeats much of Mark.

Matthew adds material that points out distinctions made between those who will be accepted into the kingdom and those who will not (Matt 24:40–25:46). Hope for the final judgment lies in how Christians make use of present life (Matt 25:31–46).

Is there any way of penetrating the heart of a document—of any document!—except on the assumption that its spirit will speak to our spirit through the actual written words?
—Karl Barth

III.7
Revelation 1–3

Assignment Objectives

To enable students:

1. To become aware of the social, historical, geographical, and religious situation of the community for which the Book of Revelation was written.

2. To reflect upon the identity of the author.

3. To recognize the Book of Revelation as a prime example of apocalyptic literature in the Bible.

4. To describe the overall structure of the Book of Revelation and of Revelation 1–3 in particular.

5. To recognize prophetic elements present in the Book of Revelation, especially in the letters to the seven churches.

6. To understand the purpose and content of the letters to the seven churches and to identify with their situations.

7. To locate Patmos, Ephesus, Smyrna, Pergamum, Thyatira, Sardis, Philadelphia, and Laodicea on a map.

Read

Revelation 1–3; Kelly, pages 247–52; Koester, pages 1–69; EDB article: "Revelation, Book of"; "Apocalyptic Literature and the Book of Revelation: Overview," #31 in the SUPPLEMENTARY READINGS at the back of the student workbook

Rationale for Student Questions

To enable students:

1. To determine key points about the Book of Revelation directly from the biblical text.
2. To identify portraits of both God and Christ given in the Book of Revelation.
3. To recognize essential elements of the letters to the churches.
4. To apply the message of the letters to their parish communities and their own lives.
5. To summarize what they have learned thus far about apocalyptic literature.

Suggested Lecture Topics

- Author of the Book of Revelation.
- Relationship of the author of the Book of Revelation to the authors of John's gospel and the Johannine letters.
- Historical, social, and religious situation of the community for which the Book of Revelation was written.
- Book of Revelation as a specific example of the genre of apocalyptic literature.
- Book of Revelation as an oral message presented with imaginative symbols representing the struggle between good and evil.
- Book of Revelation as prophetic (Rev 1:3).
- Various titles for God and Christ in the Book of Revelation.
- Elements of the seven letters and the message given to each church.

SUGGESTED ANSWERS FOR UNIT III.7

1. a. A prophetic book that is meant to be heard (Rev 1:3).

   b. God is the initiator and the message is revealed through Jesus Christ to an angel who delivers it to John, the author. The author then reports what he saw and gives the message to the churches (Rev 1:1-2).

   c. To reveal "what must happen soon" (Rev 1:1c) for the time is near (Rev 1:3c).

2. a. Portrait of God in Revelation 1-3:

   • One who reveals himself and the divine plan for creation (Rev 1:1).

   • The one who is, was, and is to come; the Alpha and Omega, the beginning and end (Rev 1:4-8)

   • The Lord and the almighty one (Rev 1:8)

   • The Father of Jesus (Rev 1:6; 2:28; 3:5, 21)

   • The source of life for all who remain faithful (Rev 2:7)

   • The one who is Spirit (Rev 2:7, 11, 17, 29; 3:6, 13, 22) and possesses and grants seven spirits (Rev 3:1)

   • The source of all power (Rev 2:27)

   • The judge of the works of humanity (Rev 3:2)

   • The one who is in heaven (Rev 3:12b)

   • The one who creates (Rev 3:14b)

   • The one who sits on the throne as ultimate ruler of the universe (Rev 3:21)

   b. Portrait of Jesus Christ in Revelation 1-3:

   • Faithful witness, firstborn of the dead, ruler of the kings of the earth (Rev 1:5a)

   • One who freed us from sin by his blood (Rev 1:5b)

   • One like a Son of Man (Rev 1:13a)

   • First and the last (Rev 1:17b, 2:8b)

   • Son of God (Rev 2:18b).

   • One who has the seven spirits of God (Rev 3:1b)

   • "Holy one, the true, who holds the key of David" (Rev 3:7b)

   • The "Amen, the faithful and true witness, the source of God's creation"(Rev 3:14b)

3. Answers to questions on seven Christian churches
   See chart on next page

Church	How is Christ described?	For what is the church praised?	For what is the church reproached?	What reward is promised?
Ephesus	Holds seven stars and walks through seven gold lampstands	Hard workers; do not tolerate the wicked—like the Nicolaitans; suffer for Jesus' name	Lost the love they first had	Right to eat from the tree of life in the garden of God
Smyrna	First and last; has died and came to life	Holding fast in the midst of suffering	Not reproached	Crown of life; not harmed by the second death
Pergamum	Has a sharp two-edged sword	Have not denied their faith	Some hold to teaching of Balaam and the Nicolaitans	Hidden manna; an inscribed white amulet
Thyatira	Son of God with eyes like a flame and feet like brass	Works, love, faith, service, and endurance	Tolerate Jezebel	Will not be burdened; given authority over nations; morning star
Sardis	Has seven spirits and seven stars	Not praised	They are dead	Dressed in white with name in book of life
Philadelphia	Holy one, true, holds the key of David, opens and closes and no one can change it	Have kept word of Jesus; not denied his name; endured	Not reproached	Kept safe in time of trial; everlasting place in the temple with name inscribed on pillar
Laodicea	Amen, faithful and true witness, source of God's creation	Not praised	Lukewarm because of riches; not needing God	Dine with Jesus and sit on his throne

III.8
Revelation 4–14

Assignment Objectives

To enable students:

1. To appreciate the theology of the Book of Revelation: who God is and the relationship between God and our world, especially in terms of God's saving victory.

2. To value the Book of Revelation for the message to its original audience.

3. To recognize how the author relates the experience of his time to that of the exodus and other scenes of salvation history.

4. To recognize the importance of Old Testament images and symbols used in the Book of Revelation.

Read

Revelation 4–14; Kelly, pages 252–57; Koester, pages 71–141; EDB article: "Beast"

Rationale for Student Questions

To enable students:
1. To trace two apocalyptic themes of the Book of Revelation.
2. To relate themes from the Book of Exodus to themes from the Book of Revelation.
3. To explore the symbolism of the woman in Revelation 12.
4. To recognize symbols used for evil in the Book of Revelation.
5. To apply apparent contradictory themes of the Bible to their own life experience.

Suggested Lecture Topics

- Apocalyptic perspective of salvation history (i.e., God's presence in the world for salvation).
- Contrast with other perspectives of salvation history (e.g., Luke).
- Old Testament background for the apocalyptic viewpoint of God's power and judgment.
- Use of the Book of Exodus by the author of the Book of Revelation.
- Representations of both good and evil in the Book of Revelation.
- Multiple symbolic meanings in the Book of Revelation.
- Apocalyptic dualisms as central to the understanding of God, the world, and self in the Book of Revelation.
- What happens in the heavens is symbolic of what happens on the earth.

John wrote [the Book of Revelation] as . . . an artist, giving to ancient images new life and meaning by combining them in the unity of a great work of art. . . . Yet it is a profoundly theological book.
—George Bradford Caird

SUGGESTED ANSWERS FOR UNIT III.8

1. God's power over creation is all-inclusive and God gives limited power for destruction: "do not damage the olive oil and the wine" (Rev 6:6c); Death and Hades have power over one-fourth of the earth (Rev 6:8); one-third of the earth (Rev 8:7b), sea (Rev 8:9), river (Rev 8:10b), heavenly beings (Rev 8:8a), and day and night (Rev 8:8b). When God judges, no one can withstand the power, not kings, generals, or the rich (Rev 6:15–17). Yet, God's abiding concern for all of creation is revealed: martyrs are given white robes (Rev 6:11a) and angels offer prayers of the saints (Rev 8:3b–4).

2. a. Revelation 4:5; 11:19 are related to the theophany on Mt. Sinai and the giving of the covenant (Exod 19:16, 24:17).

   b. Revelation 5:10 is related to God's promise to the people if they keep the covenant (Exod 19:6).

   c. Revelation 7:3 is related to the blood on the doorposts (Exod 12:7).

   d. Revelation 8:7–11 and 9:2–6 are related to
      Seventh plague, hail (Exod 9:23–26)
      First plague, water turned into blood (Exod 7:17–25)
      Ninth plague, darkness (Exod 10:21–23)
      Eighth plague, locusts (Exod 10:12–15)

   e. Revelation 12:14 is related to the eagle's wings of Exodus 19:4.

3. a. The woman's appearance is described: clothed with the sun, moon under her feet, and wearing a crown of twelve stars (Rev 12:1). The woman is pregnant, feeling birth pangs, and knows that the child she is to bear is in trouble (Rev 12:2, 4b). The woman gives birth to a male child (Rev 12:5a) before she flees into the desert, which had been prepared for her by God (Rev 12:6, 14). The woman has other children that the dragon wars against (Rev 12:17).

   b. Common interpretations of the woman described in Revelation 12:1–8 include:

      • Eve, who suffers with birth pangs (see Gen 3:15–16).

      • The Christian Church that is being persecuted (Rev 12:17).

      • Israel (Rev 12:5).

      • Tradition has associated the woman with Mary because the child is the Messiah and the Lamb (Rev 12:10–11). Revelation 12:1–6a is proclaimed from the Lectionary on the feast of the Assumption of Mary.

4. Enemies of the Christian community are symbolically represented by:

   • The great red dragon, who is identified as "the Devil and Satan, the deceiver of the whole world" (Rev 12:9a).

   • The beast from the sea, who most probably refers to the Roman Empire as embodied in its emperors. Nero is offered as the model persecutor of Christians and the current emperor, Domitian, is fashioned after this model. Receives power from the dragon (Rev 13:2b).

   • The beast from the earth, who most likely represents a false prophet who acts for the Roman Empire as its delegate in Asia Minor and demands total allegiance to Rome, perhaps encouraging emperor worship.

III.9
Revelation 15–22

Assignment Objectives

To enable students:

1. To interpret Old Testament symbols in the Book of Revelation.

2. To see the relationship between the theology of the Book of Revelation and the social tensions of the Christian community in the first century.

3. To note that God's relationship with us is an important key to the interpretation of the Book of Revelation.

4. To identify how the Book of Revelation presents God as victorious over all evil.

5. To be aware of the message of hope that the author wishes to give the Christian community.

6. To summarize the picture of both God and Jesus as given in the Book of Revelation.

7. To recognize that the message and theology of the Book of Revelation can be correctly understood only in relation to the whole Bible.

Read
Revelation 15–22; Kelly, pages 257–59; Koester, pages 141–205; EDB articles: "Exile," "Millennium," and "Scroll"

Rationale for Student Questions

To enable students:

1. To reflect on the author's choice of symbols by examining the links connecting them to the author's historical situation and knowledge of the Old Testament.
2. To deepen their understanding of the identity of Jesus as presented in Revelation 19:11–16.
3. To reflect on the different images of the last judgment as found in Matthew and in Revelation and how they complement one another.
4. To connect the last book of the Bible (Revelation) to the first book of the Bible (Genesis).
5. To grasp the hopefulness that the author of the Book of Revelation wishes to leave with the Christian community.
6. To appreciate the Book of Revelation in a new way and to connect it to contemporary religious movements.

Suggested Lecture Topics

- God as central focus of revelation.
- God's actions regarding the judgment of nations, in particular Babylon as symbolic of Rome, both of which destroyed the Jerusalem temple.
- Concluding work with symbols and understanding their meaning in a broader context.
- How some letters from Greek and Hebrew alphabets represent numerical values.
- Symbolic use of numbers in the Book of Revelation.
- The last judgment as an expression of Christian truth about God, the world, and humanity.
- The New Jerusalem as symbol of the triumph of good over evil.
- The Book of Revelation in the context of the whole of biblical revelation.

SUGGESTED ANSWERS FOR UNIT III.9

1. Babylon had taken Judah into exile after the destruction of the first Jerusalem temple in 587 BC. Likewise, in AD 70, the Romans destroyed the second Jerusalem temple. The mighty Babylon had warred against God's people and had fallen prey to other great empires. So, too, the biblical author hopes that the mighty Rome, having warred against God's people, will fall prey to a greater power.

2. a. Jesus is the faithful and true judge (Rev 19:11), the Word of God (Rev 19:13b), the "King of kings and Lord of Lords" (Rev 19:16).

   b. The works that Jesus does are: judge (Rev 19:11c), strike down enemies (Rev 19:15a), rule with a rod of iron (Rev 19:15b), and dispense the wrath of God upon the enemies of the Christian community (Rev 19:15c). The impression portrayed in the text is that Jesus will never be conquered. He is the ultimate ruler of all.

3.

Comparison	Revelation 20:11–15	Matthew 25:31–46
Judge	Apparently, God, even though not specifically stated	Son of Man (25:31)
Who is judged	All the dead (20:12)	All the nations (25:32)
Judgment seat	Throne of God (20:12a)	Throne the Son of Man has won (25:31b)
Criteria for judgment	Name written in the book of life and person's recorded deeds (20:12-13)	Specific actions toward the lowly and those in need (25:35–36)
Salvation result	No explicit indication of fate of those whose names appear in book of life. However, Revelation 21 speaks of the eternal blessedness of the saints.	Inherit the kingdom prepared by the Father from all time (25:34)
Condemnation result	Thrown into the lake of fire (20:15b)	Go to eternal punishment (25:46a)

4. Some passages in Revelation 22 reminiscent of the Garden of Eden account in Genesis:

   - The river rises and flows throughout (Rev 22:1-2; Gen. 2:10-14).

   - The tree of life (Rev 22:2; Gen 2:9).

   - Fruit of the trees (Rev 22:2; Gen 2:9, 16; 3:2).

   - God is present (Rev 22:3; Gen 2:4b-26); nothing accursed in the place (Rev 22:3; implied in Gen 2:4b-26).

   - Warning of the truth of God's words and commands (Rev 22:7-19; Gen 2-3 [throughout]).

   - Those who do not obey God's word and accept God's actions on their behalf lose the share in the tree of life (Rev 22:14, 19; Gen 3:22-24).

III.10
Unit Three Review

Students will be responsible for:

1. A memory verse from John's gospel, one of the Johannine letters, or the Book of Revelation, indicating the translation used and citing reference.

2. The information included in the following SUPPLEMENTARY READINGS at the back of the student workbook:
   #24. "The Gospel According to John and the Johannine Letters: Overview"
   #29. "Self-Quiz on John's Gospel and the Johannine Letters"
   #31. "Apocalyptic Literature and the Book of Revelation: Overview"
   #32. "Self-Quiz on the Book of Revelation"

3. The location of the following places and areas on a map.

Bethany	Galilee
Bethsaida	Judea
Cana	Samaria
Capernaum	Sea of Tiberias (John's name for Sea of Galilee)
Dead Sea	Sychar

Suggested Lecture Topics

- Review the basic information on John's gospel, stressing its context, unique structure, theology, themes, and its independence from the synoptic traditions.
- Review the basic information on the Johannine letters, emphasizing their context, structure, theology, and themes.
- Review the genre and theology of apocalyptic literature.
- Review the basic information on the Book of Revelation, stressing its context, literary genre, theology, and themes. Note that the Book of Revelation must be integrated into the rest of the Bible for an adequate interpretation.
- Review geography.

Students express their appreciation to the members of their study group

The aim of this exercise is for students to express their appreciation for the members of their small group for this year.

Each student:

1. Takes the name of one person in the small group. (Each group makes sure that all members have a name; absent members should be contacted.)

2. Writes a brief testimonial about the gift that person's presence has been to the group during this year. Perhaps a guideline could be this message from Paul to the Ephesians (4:25–32 in part):

   So then, putting away falsehood, let all of us speak the truth to our neighbors, for we are members of one another...Let no evil talk come out of your mouths, but only what is useful for building up, as there is need, so that your words may give grace to those who hear...and be kind to one another, tenderhearted, forgiving one another, as God in Christ has forgiven you.

3. Brings the testimonial the following week, shares it with the group, and then presents it to the person about whom he or she wrote.

Since students will be in different groups next year, they should reflect upon the fact that new insights about their faith journey this year have come not only from their personal study, but also from working together in their group week after week. They should also take to heart the words of the U.S. bishops' letter on evangelization, *Go and Make Disciples* (1992):

   Conversion is the change of our lives which comes about through the power of the Holy Spirit. All who accept the Gospel undergo a change as we continually put on the mind of Christ by rejecting sin and becoming more faithful disciples in the church. Unless we undergo conversion, we have not truly accepted the Gospel.

Name _____

Center _____ Group # _____

1. How would you describe John's purpose in writing his gospel?

2. How would you characterize the portrait of Jesus in John's gospel?

3. How would you characterize the portrait of Christian discipleship in John's gospel?

4. Briefly explain what you consider to be the most important theme in John's gospel.

5. Briefly explain the purpose of apocalyptic literature.

6. How would you characterize the portrait of Jesus in the Book of Revelation?

7. How would you characterize the portrait of Christian discipleship in the Book of Revelation?

8. Briefly explain what you consider to be the most important theme in the Book of Revelation.

9. What is the most significant thing you have learned during your study of John, the Johannine letters, and the Book of Revelation?

10. Write your memory verse from John, the Johannine letters, or the Book of Revelation. Include reference and translation used.

MAP

I. Write the number of each of the following places next to the appropriate dot on the map:

1. Bethany
2. Bethsaida
3. Cana
4. Capernaum
5. Sychar

II. Indicate on the map where the following are located:

Dead Sea

Galilee

Judea

Samaria

Sea of Tiberias

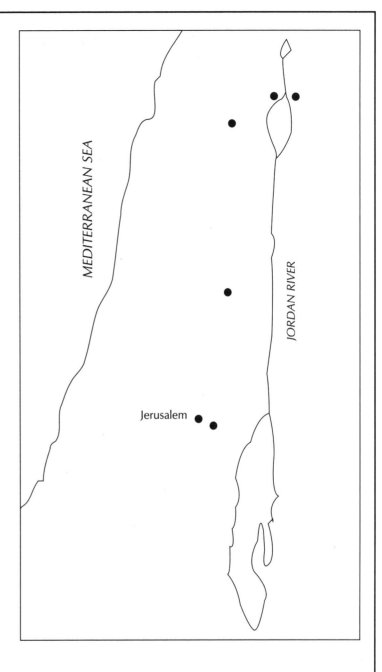

Bonus Questions:

1. Where was John when he received the visions described in the Book of Revelation?

2. List the seven churches John addressed in the Book of Revelation.

ANSWERS TO YEAR TWO–UNIT THREE TEST

1. The purpose of John's gospel is stated within the gospel itself: "That you may come to believe that Jesus is the Messiah, the Son of God, and that through believing you may have life in his name" (John 20:31).

2. Jesus is the revealer of God (the divine Word) and the divine Son sent for salvation. There are other possibilities.

3. Some characteristics of the Christian disciple in John are that the disciple is intimate with Jesus, recognizes Jesus, really understands Jesus because of the love they share; believes that Jesus is the resurrection and the life and recognizes the Risen Lord as being present in the midst of the community; consumes the flesh and blood of Jesus; follows Jesus to the cross as a member of the community of faith; accepts and works through the power of the Advocate.

4. Many possibilities; consult "The Gospel According to John and the Johannine Letters: Overview," #24 in the SUPPLEMENTARY READINGS at the back of the student workbook.

5. Apocalyptic literature tries to: give hope in a time of crisis; strengthen the faith (trust) of God's people under trial in anticipation of the final and decisive intervention of God for salvation; provide consolation by recognizing God's sovereignty and judgment of evil.

6. Jesus is the faithful witness; firstborn from the dead; the Lamb that was slain for the salvation of all; Lord of lords and King of kings; judge of all creation. There are other possibilities.

7. Some characteristics of the Christian disciple in the Book of Revelation are that the disciple remains faithful and worships God no matter what the cost; perseveres and is hopeful in the victory of God; turns from complacency and compromise; places trust in God alone; hears and keeps what is written in the prophetic words.

8. Many possibilities; consult "Apocalyptic Literature and the Book of Revelation: Overview," #31 in the SUPPLEMENTARY READINGS at the back of the student workbook.

9. Many possibilities; note what impressed students the most. This might provide clues for what to emphasize the next time you present this material.

10. Any passage from John's gospel, the Johannine letters, or the Book of Revelation. Reference and translation used must be included.

MAP

I. North (left to right): 3. (Cana); 4.(Capernaum); 2. (Bethsaida)

Center: 5. (Sychar)

South: 1. (Bethany)

II. The three areas in north-to-south order are Galilee, Samaria, Judea.
    (Consult the Hammond Atlas for exact locations)

The sea in the north is the Sea of Tiberius (also known as the Sea of Galilee).

The sea in the south is the Dead Sea.

BONUS QUESTIONS

1. Patmos

2. (In any order) Ephesus, Smyrna, Pergamum, Thyatira, Sardis, Philadelphia, Laodicea

FOUR-YEAR PLAN OF STUDY IN THE CATHOLIC BIBLICAL SCHOOL

UNITS	BIBLICAL BOOKS	THEOLOGICAL THEMES	GENERAL ISSUES
FIRST YEAR: OLD TESTAMENT FOUNDATIONS — GENESIS THROUGH KINGS			
UNIT 1	Exodus Leviticus Numbers	People of God Covenant Desert	Sources of the Pentateuch
UNIT 2	Deuteronomy Genesis	Promise/The Land Creation/Sin	Form Criticism Fertile Crescent
UNIT 3	Joshua Judges 1 and 2 Samuel 1 and 2 Kings	Charismatic Leadership Kingship Prophecy	Geography of Palestine Canaanite Religion Biblical Chronology Biblical Archeology
SECOND YEAR: NEW TESTAMENT FOUNDATIONS — JESUS AND DISCIPLESHIP			
UNIT 1	Mark Luke Matthew 1 and 2	Discipleship Holy Spirit Infancy Narratives	Synoptic Question Form Criticism Redaction Criticism
UNIT 2	Acts Pauline Letters	Church Gifts of the Holy Spirit	New Testament Geography Letter as Literary Form
UNIT 3	John and Johannine Letters Mark 13, Luke 21 Matthew 24—25 Revelation	Sacraments Eschatology	Apocalyptic Writing
THIRD YEAR: OLD TESTAMENT CONTINUED — EXILE AND RESTORATION			
UNIT 1	Amos Hosea 1 Isaiah Micah Zephaniah Nahum Jeremiah	Social Justice Prophetic Vocation Marriage of God and Israel	Biblical Chronology
UNIT 2	Lamentations Obadiah Ezekiel 2 Isaiah Haggai Zechariah 1—8 3 Isaiah Ezra Nehemiah	Destruction of the Temple Meaning of the Exile Renewal after Exile Community Rebuilt around the Word	Crisis of the Exile Strategies of Renewal
UNIT 3	1 and 2 Chronicles Joel Malachi Zechariah 9-14 Ruth Song of Songs Psalms	Rebuilding a People Importance of the Law	Historical Writings of Old Testament Hebrew Poetry Jewish Liturgy
FOURTH YEAR: BOTH TESTAMENTS CONCLUDED — THE WORD IN THE HELLENISTIC WORLD			
UNIT 1	Proverbs Habakkuk Job Ecclesiastes Sirach Wisdom	Creation Emphasis Problem of Suffering	Priest, Prophet, and Sage
UNIT 2	Jonah Esther Tobit Baruch 1 and 2 Maccabees Judith Daniel	 Martyrdom Resurrection	Deuterocanonical Books Hellenism

UNIT 3	Matthew
	Pastoral Letters
	Catholic Letters
	Hebrews
		Role of Peter/Apostles
		New Testament as Fulfillment
		    of Old Testament
			Christianity as a New Form of Religion
			    in the Roman World